Technical Training Basics

Sarah Wakefield

ASTD
PRESS

Alexandria, Virginia

ASTD Press is an internationally renowned source of insightful and practical information on workplace learning and performance topics, including training basics, evaluation and return on investment, instructional systems development, e-learning, leadership, and career development. Visit us at www.astd.org/astdpress.

Ordering information: Books published by ASTD Press can be purchased by visiting ASTD's website at store.astd.org or by calling 800.628.2783 or 703.683.8100.

Library of Congress Control Number: 2010938802

ISBN-10: 1-56286-755-5
ISBN-13: 978-1-56286-755-3

ASTD Press Editorial Staff:
Director: Anthony Allen
Manager, ASTD Press: Larry Fox
Community Manager, Learning Technologies: Justin Brusino
Associate Editor: Ashley McDonald
Editorial Assistant: Stephanie Castellano
Copyediting, Interior Design, and Production: Abella Publishing Services, LLC
Cover Design: Ana Foreman

Printed by Versa Press, Inc., East Peoria, IL, www.versapress.com

Contents

About the
Training Basics Series

▪▪▪

ASTD's *Training Basics* series recognizes and, in many ways, celebrates the fast-paced, ever-changing reality of organizations today. Jobs, roles, and expectations change quickly. One day you might be a network administrator or a process line manager, and the next day you might be asked to train 50 employees in basic computer skills or to instruct line workers in quality processes.

Where do you turn for help? The ASTD *Training Basics* series is designed to be your one-stop solution. The series takes a minimalist approach to your learning curve dilemma and presents only the information you need to be successful. Each book in the series guides you through key aspects of training: giving presentations, making the transition to the role of trainer, designing and delivering training, and evaluating training. The books in the series also include some advanced skills such as performance and basic business proficiencies.

The ASTD *Training Basics* series is the perfect tool for training and performance professionals looking for easy-to-understand materials that will prepare non-trainers to take on a training role. In addition, this series is the perfect reference tool for any trainer's bookshelf and a quick way to hone your existing skills.

Preface

When industrial accidents occur as a result of human error, it is only a matter of time before the inevitable question is asked: Where was the training?

In a world where things like safety, quality, and efficiency are essential, we cannot afford ineffective, inefficient technical training. Technical training must be done, and it must be done well in today's business environment.

Yet, with all that said, there are few resources available that specifically discuss how to effectively develop technical training.

Technical training development is a complex, challenging, unique, misunderstood, and sometimes frustrating process. As a nontechnical course developer, your job is especially tricky: You must complete all the regular tasks of developing courseware, but you must do this using words and concepts you don't fully understand.

I have worked with contract course developers from all different levels, including developers who were paid a premium for their impressive (on paper, at least) backgrounds. But what I have learned from this is that experience isn't always the biggest success factor for putting together a technical course. Some of the most expensive, experienced developers have let me down—calling me one week before an assignment is due to tell me that the project is just too complicated for them, that they have never had to do anything so difficult before, and that they won't be able to finish. Conversely, I have worked with developers fresh out of college who demonstrated specific promising skills and with a little practice were able to produce efficiently and outperform other, more experienced individuals.

I've noticed that the technical developers who are successful all exhibit some of the same characteristics and approaches. That is what this book is about.

Technical training requires different tactics to develop than nontechnical training. One of the biggest success factors of technical training development is being able to work effectively with your subject matter expert (SME). In addition, launching the project the right way, understanding different ways technical courses can be organized, finding the right information, designing technical exercises, and piloting a course with an SME/instructor are all important items to know. This book is intended to discuss these things and more—in a very real, specific, and readable way.

What This Book Does Not Cover

If you have never designed a training class before, this book is not for you. This book does not go into great depth on *why* things like the ADDIE model and adult learning are necessary; rather, it covers how to *apply* those concepts to a *technical* training project. It is expected that you already understand the basic tenets of instructional design and adult learning tactics.

Primary Audience

The primary audience of this book is anyone who develops technical training with the help of an SME. This includes training developers, instructional designers, curriculum developers, technical writers, training managers, training coordinators, content designers, and training specialists, among others.

SMEs who develop their own technical training will still be able to pull concepts from this book, but the bulk of the writing is geared toward developers who are working with an SME.

Chapter-by-Chapter Highlights

This book provides specific ideas, tips, and strategies to effectively and efficiently develop technical training, from the beginning of the project all the way through the pilot course and postcourse review. This book is loosely organized according to the course development process. Specifically, the chapters cover the following:

Chapter 1: The Technical Training Enigma describes technical training and discusses some of the differences between technical and nontechnical training. The technical organization is briefly explored.

Chapter 2: The Successful Development Team covers the roles needed for technical course development and the characteristics of an effective developer and an SME.

Chapter 3: Beginning the Technical Training Project discusses aspects related to the initial course design meeting, including why the meeting is important, who should attend, important questions to ask, and what should be accomplished.

Chapter 4: Arranging a Technical Course describes how to create a course design document. The chapter examines in detail the various options available for arranging a technical products or task-based course.

Chapter 5: Gathering Information discusses the type of information to seek and the challenges associated with gathering technical data. Potential in-house and outside sources of data are explored. The chapter analyzes tactics for maximizing information received, along with organizational systems for the technical designer.

Chapter 6: Working with Subject Matter Experts covers tangible ways to draw information out of SMEs. The chapter gives specific tips for going through edits with SMEs.

Chapter 7: Designing Classroom Exercises for Highly Technical Content provides specific examples, templates, and takeaways of exercises designed for highly technical content. The chapter also covers the importance of building a library of examples.

Chapter 8: The Pilot Class and Beyond explores development opportunities from the pilot class, helping out the SME-turned-trainer, and postcourse maintenance.

Chapter 9: Troubleshooting: Challenges and Solutions investigates different technical training challenges and provides specific and useful takeaways and solutions.

Look for These Icons

What's Inside This Chapter

Each chapter of the book begins with a preview of the topics discussed in the chapter. You can use this information as a guide for what to expect as well as a quick reference should you wish to jump to a section that interests you most.

Think About This

These sections consist of specific lists, tips, and questions that will help you utilize the techniques and concepts covered in the chapter.

Basic Rules

These rules are short statements that encompass the important and fundamental tenets of technical training development.

Noted

These sections include important additional information that slightly digresses from the regular text.

Getting It Done

This is the final section of each chapter. This section provides a way for you to relate the concepts and principles to your own technical training project.

Acknowledgments

I would like to thank my husband, John, for all of his support, edits, and comprehensive insights for this book. His intelligence, care, and patience were wonderful during the process. I would also like to thank my daughter, Marie, for her humor and smile that make my day. Finally, thank you to the professionals quoted in this book. Your contributions added much-appreciated perspective and made the finished product much more valuable.

The Technical Training Enigma

What's Inside This Chapter

In this chapter, you'll learn

▶ what technical training is
▶ the differences between technical and nontechnical training
▶ what a technical organization is
▶ the role of technical training within the technical organization.

How do you develop training for a specialized, complex subject that you don't fully understand? This feat is accomplished daily by technical training developers all over the world. Technical training can be a mystery. An early experience opened my eyes to this:

I stare at the scribbled notes in front of me. My engineer co-worker has just given them to me so I can incorporate them into a training manual I am developing.

Make up your bottom hole assembly on the rig floor and trip in the hole. Apply weight until the pin shears and the whipstock anchor sets. Mill your window and watch your flow rate. Drill the rathole. POOH. Write up Post Job Report.

Wait, POOH? *You can't be serious*, I say to myself. What does that even *mean*? I reread the paragraph. This is one of my first big assignments as a curriculum developer for an oil field service company. I know I need to figure this out somehow. I read the paragraph again.

"You look confused."

I look up and see my engineer co-worker standing in my doorway. "Do you have a question?" he asks.

I hesitate and then blurt awkwardly, "What is POOH?" He looks confused, and I quickly add, "What does the acronym P-O-O-H stand for?"

Laughter. "It stands for **P**ull **O**ut **o**f **H**ole, as in when you are taking equipment out of the ground," he says, a smile on his face.

"Oh," I say. "Of course it does."

■ ■ ■ ■ ■

Nowadays the "POOH" warning is one of the first things I bring up to my new technical writers. I don't mention it to show my lack of technical knowledge, and I don't mention it because saying "POOH" in front of a group of people is a great icebreaker. The story highlights the fundamental challenge of technical training: the Technical Training Enigma.

The Technical Training Enigma gets at the essence of what is difficult about technical training development. As a nontechnical course developer, you are doubly challenged: You must complete all the regular challenges of writing and putting together courseware, but you must do it by using words and concepts you don't fully understand.

It is a process that can be astonishingly frustrating. If you are unable to crack this enigma, you lower your chances for success, and a poor work product can result.

There do exist strategies, tips, and tricks that can be used effectively to develop technical training, but before we delve into cracking this enigma, we must first address the basics: definitions and descriptions of terms that will be used throughout this book. We'll start with the most basic question of all.

What Is Technical Training?

Technical training is instruction based on a technical product or a technical task. A technical product is something marketed or sold whose worth is determined by scientific, engineering, mathematical, or design principles. In other words, a technical product is a commodity that will assist in carrying out mechanical, production-related, scientific, or engineering tasks. Technical products include everything from tools, equipment, electronics, computer programs, devices, and instruments to gizmos, thingamajigs, widgets, and doodads.

Technical tasks include services, procedures, or jobs performed using a technical product. Technical tasks can be anything from repairing an HVAC system to running a lab spectrometer to designing an oil field drill bit to performing routine maintenance on a military tank engine.

So, for example, a centrifuge machine is considered a technical product. Related technical tasks might include the ways to assemble, disassemble, load, test, unload, maintain, operate, or troubleshoot the centrifuge machine.

Basic Rule

Technical training is training based on a technical product or task.

Technical training can proceed along one of three avenues, depending on whether its focus is on technical products, technical tasks, or a combination of both. So, for example, your training class could cover just the internal components and functioning of a machine (a technical products course), it could cover only how to operate that machine (a technical tasks course), or it could cover both (a combination technical products and tasks course). It is important that you identify which of these areas your technical topic encompasses, as this will affect future decisions you make about the course.

Noted

Technical courses tend to have a primary target audience of individuals who will actually be working with or operating the products or equipment. This does not mean that these people already have operational experience. But, as part of their job description, they deal (or someday will be expected to deal) with highly specialized and complicated technical products or tasks. Examples of common target audiences for technical training courses include engineers, technicians, operators, programmers, doctors, researchers, mechanics, and inspectors.

Differences Between Technical and Nontechnical Training

While they do share some similarities, technical training and nontechnical training are quite different. Nontechnical training deals with soft skills such as leadership, management, conflict, public speaking, time management, project management, and so on.

Technical training is not as easily classified. For example, the content you would gather if you were developing an interpersonal communication skills course would be more or less the same whether you were teaching in a biomedical research lab or a big manufacturing center. However, the technical training content you would gather if you were designing technical courses for one of those places would be unique. In many instances, the course you develop will be the first of its kind. Whereas nontechnical content is more likely to apply across the board, technical content is specialized and specific to each topic.

Technical training topics usually have at least one of the following characteristics:

- A distinct vocabulary is used.
- Existing information and resources are scarce or solely experience based.
- It takes years to learn the intricacies of the topic.
- Available information is often proprietary.
- The product in question is in a state of development.
- Because it deals with complex and complicated topics, the technical training takes longer to develop.

Another significant—if not the most significant—difference between nontechnical and technical training is that technical training development is extremely dependent on *subject matter experts*. Because technical courses are designed based on the information given by a subject matter expert (SME), we are inherently dependent on the SME when designing a course. In fact, as the topics get more complicated, the instructional design "secret" becomes more about productive communication with your SME. Being able to draw information from an SME becomes a critical skill for a nontechnical designer developing a highly technical training course.

As you proceed through this book, you will find that developing your relationship with the SME and your ability to understand and comprehend information the SME gives you are among the most important skills you can have. Reliance on the SME marks one of the most fundamental differences between nontechnical training and technical training. The SME is the foundation for deciphering the Technical Training Enigma; cracking the enigma begins and ends with the SME.

What Is a Technical Organization?

In this age of multinational, multi-industrial, global omni-companies, it can be difficult to come up with one single definition of a technical organization. One way to define it is to look at whom the organization employs. Are the majority of its employees technicians, scientists, or engineers? If so, there is a good chance that the organization is technically based. There is also the obvious description of a technical organization as "an organization that deals with technology;" however, such a broad definition certainly does not describe the kind of work the organization does. Instead, consider this definition submitted by a professional who works with and for technical organizations:

> *A technical organization is any organization that creates or distributes technology to the consumer. This includes engineering and design organizations, including Research and Development (R&D) departments of large businesses, as well as the organizations that apply technology through the manufacture and implementation of tools, techniques, and systems.*
>
> *So, a technical organization is any group that designs, makes, or sells anything complex.*
> —Stefanie Matta, Contract Technical Writer, Houston, Texas

This description provides a broad, but accurate, picture of what a technical organization is.

The Role of Technical Training Within the Technical Organization

Effective technical training is essential to the technical organization. Consider the following quotes:

> *In an age when Quality, Health, Safety, and Environmental Impact have become a focus at all levels, we cannot afford to ignore technical training, which is essential to safe and efficient operations.*
> —Bob Taylor, Founder, Taylormade Training Consultants, Perth, Australia

Effective, cost-controlled training is an absolute. Inefficiencies are not allowed. Time in class must produce learning or it and your coursework will eventually be eliminated. In short, bad training that produces little or no results will not endure today's business environment.

—Kenny Amend, Hub Manager, Weatherford International, Houston, Texas

In the cutthroat world of today's marketplace, there is no room for accidents, there is no room for quality control failures, and there is no room for inefficiency. Every technical product and technical service is produced and distributed under a microscope. Just by watching the news, you can see the catastrophic consequences that result if personnel dealing with technology are not adequately prepared. Following are some of the outputs of quality technical training.

Accident Prevention

One constant is that technical organizations face more risk of catastrophic accidents than do nontechnical organizations. For example, imagine a lawyer who mistypes a word versus an air-traffic controller software engineer who mistypes a word. What if a salesman skips a few steps in his sales call? How about a nuclear plant operator who skips a few steps in his processes?

For technical companies that deal with potentially dangerous equipment or services, effective training is absolutely essential. Nothing will torpedo a company faster than a disaster that could have been avoided by better training. Industrial companies lose people to accidents every year; it is inconceivable that such companies would settle for anything less than the best training available.

Cost Savings

How many man-hours could be saved if classroom training was as efficient as it could be? How often are participants allowed to mentally check out of training classes because of poor instructional structure? How many mistakes are made, or how many hours of productivity are lost, when someone must relearn on the job what he or she should have learned in class?

A lean, efficient company simply cannot afford to use old methods of training.

Quality of Product

When an organization's employees are highly trained, the entire corporation benefits. Employees are then equipped with the knowledge and information to make informed choices on the job. The reliability of the product or service becomes established. The efficiency of the company pleases stockholders and investors. The company stays out of the newspaper disaster headlines.

A company can be truly enhanced and supported by its training department. For these reasons, good technical training is absolutely essential.

Noted

In some technical organizations, you may find that several people within the technical training departments have little formal experience with educational research and training design. These training departments will be staffed with experienced technicians or engineers who have proven expertise in the field, but not necessarily in the classroom. In these training departments, the lack of effective instructional or curriculum design has one telltale sign: the 100 percent lecture class. Every class you see will consist solely of a lecture, typically with some derivative of a PowerPoint presentation.

The 100 percent lecture-based training is not a sign of laziness or lack of imagination. A lot of engineering and "hard sciences" programs in American universities are still primarily lecture based. Technical people who attended these schools and graduated with these majors will often default to reproduce the education they experienced, often unaware that new advances in educational technology have occurred. (Chapter 7, "Designing Classroom Exercises for Highly Technical Content," will touch more on the research that backs up modern training and an active classroom.)

Your job will be to bring your technical organization's training out of the nineteenth-century lecture and into the twenty-first-century interactive classroom.

What We've Learned

The Technical Training Enigma gets at the essence of what is difficult about technical training development. As a nontechnical course developer, your job is especially challenging: You must develop courseware using words and concepts you don't fully understand.

It is certainly demanding, but the first step of solving the Technical Training Enigma is to gain an understanding of the basics of technical training. In this chapter, we saw that technical training deals with a technical product or task, and that the differences between nontechnical and technical training are distinct. (Technical training has its own set of challenges!) A technical organization is any group that designs, makes, or sells anything complex. In a world where quality, health, safety, and the environment are integral to business, effective training is a must.

The Technical Training Enigma will always exist, but there are specific tips, tricks, and tactics that can help ease you along the way. With preparation and a mastery of the processes and strategies contained in this book, you can meet your own technical training challenge with effectiveness.

Getting It Done

Understanding the technical organization within which you are working will help you to be more efficient in finishing your training development project.

Worksheet 1–1. My Technical Training Project

Answer the following questions to help you analyze your own technical training project.

1. Is my class a technical products class, a technical tasks class, or a combination of both?

2. What are some characteristics of the technical organization with which I am currently working? What is the culture? What are the norms? What are the backgrounds of the people I will be working with during this training project?

2

The Successful Development Team

What's Inside This Chapter

In this chapter, you'll learn

▶ the roles required for technical course development
▶ successful developer characteristics
▶ ideal SME traits
▶ how to find a good SME.

Building a strong development team for your technical training course is a necessity. Each role in the team is important and ensures that the perspectives required for a complete project are represented. When the right people are in place, all components of the project are covered.

Roles in Technical Course Development

In the technical course development world, there are two different but equally important sides of the spectrum. On one side is the instructional segment, which encompasses course structure, organization, and learning theory. The other side is the technical segment, which comprises the technical content within the course structure. Without one segment, the final product would be incomplete. Both sides must work together to produce a successful course.

Figure 2–1. Two Sides of a Successful Course

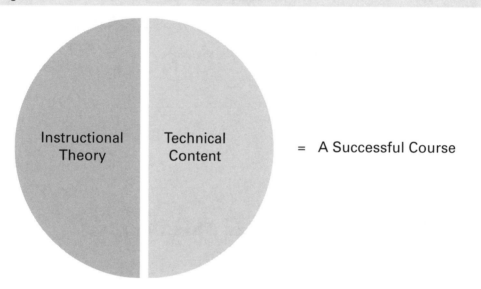

Corresponding to these two sides of the spectrum are two distinct roles required for a course development project: the developer and the subject matter expert (SME). As their names imply, the developer offers expertise on the instructional side of the course, and the SME offers expertise on the technical side. The SME has the final say in "what" is said during the course, and the developer has the final say in "how" it is said.

Basic Rule

The developer is in charge of the instructional theory and structure of the course; the SME is in charge of the technical course content.

An individual carrying out the instructional role may have a job title such as instructional designer, training specialist, technical writer, or content developer, among a number of other titles. An individual carrying out the technical role might be an engineer, an equipment operator, a technical trainer, a technician, a programmer, a physician, a researcher, or one of an entire host of other professionals. What the individual job titles might be within each role or how many people end up fulfilling each role is not important. What is important is that *both the developer and SME roles* be filled within the course development team. It is vital that both roles be given respect and that they contribute equally to the outcome. Both roles have distinct and essential responsibilities during the project.

The Developer . . .

structures content so that it appeals to several different learning preferences and takes into account numerous methods of instruction.

The SME . . .

provides technical content, ensures that terminology is used correctly, and that the entire topic is represented accurately.

The Developer . . .

structures course objectives in a SMART (Specific, Measurable, Achievable, Realistic, and Testable) format.

The SME . . .

provides assurance that the objectives are relevant to the target audience's job.

The Developer . . .

wants an organization with a logical flow that is easy to follow based on how learners' memories work.

The SME . . .

wants an organization with a logical flow that is consistent with the intricacies of the technical topic.

The Developer . . .

formats the training material to utilize correct grammar, spelling, and punctuation.

The SME . . .

makes certain that the document reads correctly according to "regular" industry jargon.

Noted

There is no reason that the developer and the SME cannot be the same person. In some instances, both roles are included in one job description. However, even if one person fulfills both roles, it is still extremely important that each role be given its distinct due diligence.

Success in the development of a technical course begins with ensuring that the important roles of the development team are present. The *next* step involves filling those roles *effectively*. The next two sections describe the characteristics of the successful developer and the ideal SME.

Successful Developer Characteristics

Successful developers share a few common characteristics, such as good communication skills, adaptability, and the desire to understand a complicated topic. These and other important traits will be explained below. As you read the section, keep in mind that understanding and striving for each of these qualities can help you become more effective as a developer.

Utilizes Good People Skills

An effective developer must communicate well so that everyone on the team will understand what is required, how the project is proceeding, and any issues that need to be addressed. Your good communication skills should apply to all sorts of people. SMEs come with different nationalities, genders, personalities, and even egos. Remember that there are times with technical training that, to do your job, you are almost solely dependent on your SME. If you alienate your SME with a rude comment, he or she is less likely to work well with you, thus thwarting both your efforts. As one with a great stake in the relationship, you should be adept at reading your SME and anticipating how he or she prefers to work. If you can aptly tap into your SME's working style and communication preferences, you will have a better chance of drawing out the needed technical information and completing the development project.

Doesn't Give Up Easily

It is easier said than done, but an effective developer does not give up on a project at the first sign of adversity. Technical topics can be quite difficult. Try to avoid becoming discouraged if you don't fully understand a topic after an hour, two weeks, or three months. It takes people years to become experts on a subject; keeping this in mind and persevering despite frustration gives you a better chance of success.

Asks Questions

Being fearless when it comes to asking questions is perhaps the most obvious quality an effective developer needs. Clearly, as a non-expert on a complicated topic, you are going to have questions and you are going to have a lot of them. You may have to endure strange looks from your SME when you ask yet another question, but you need to have thick skin. You must be able to continue asking questions until you find the answer you need.

Is a Good Listener

Now that you understand the power of opening your mouth to ask questions, don't underestimate the simple power of closing your mouth to listen! Sometimes your SME will say things you won't find documented in any other source, and for many technical topics, your SME can hold all the answers you need to finish a class. Successful developers understand this and pay close attention when an SME starts spouting jargon and talking shop.

Applies Knowledge of Instructional Design

An effective developer has a solid work foundation. You should understand the basic tenets of the instructional design process and utilize these major steps as you develop your courses. This is often learned over several years of work in the industry; however, classes (and books!) may make your knowledge base much broader.

Draws upon a Sense of Humor

Don't be afraid to see the lighter side of all this technical stuff. SMEs often spout off uproariously funny technical jargon, oblivious to how they sound to the untrained ear. Your audience will, in all likelihood, find the same jargon as funny as you do upon hearing it the first time. You can *use* that in your training development to great success. In addition, you should also be able to laugh at yourself. As novices with the technical material, we will from time to time make mistakes and confuse a "shale dome" with a "salt dome," an "RCD" with an "RDC," or an "*overused* overshot guide" with an "*oversized* overshot guide." SMEs sometimes chortle at our humorously incorrect (but certainly rational) interpretations of technical data. As a developer, you need to keep your perspective. If you can see the humor in a situation and laugh at yourself, you are likely to go further.

Desires to Understand a Complicated Topic

Mighty is the developer who desires to truly understand a complicated technical topic. This person is not OK with just a one-word cursory answer given by an SME. This person asks "why" a hundred times, not because he or she is tedious, but because he or she is truly interested in bettering his or her understanding of the topic. When you are really trying to learn something, you will ask the natural questions that a new learner will ask. These questions will be useful to the course development process because, as a learner, you can help the SME realize that certain aspects of the topic might be important to someone without the SME's level of expertise. Sometimes, the SME will see how you are internalizing the topic, which will highlight additional or specific areas on which the course should focus.

Accepts Criticism

There is nothing truer than the adage "Everyone makes mistakes." You should be able to take any criticism you receive in stride and use it to improve yourself. As you go through the development and editing process, your content will many times be completely crossed out and marked up by your SME. Don't become so attached to what you have created that you are not able to separate yourself from it. You should be highly vested in the material as you craft it, but once that material goes for review, you need to be able to look at the edits from an outside perspective, as if you were not the person who spent the last 17 sleepless nights trying to crank the project out. Don't be easily offended, and your development life will be easier.

Is Adaptable

You may find that something that worked particularly well for one project and SME does not work at all for your next project. Such is the nature of technical topics and working with different SMEs. You certainly should not forget about the things that have made you successful previously, but you must be adaptable. You may have to tweak the details of your work process to fit various projects.

Requires a Quality Product

I once worked with a developer whose sole goal was to "get it done." It did not matter what the work product looked like, only that it was finished. As such, whether information was actually correct was irrelevant; this developer just wanted enough of *some kind* of information to fill up a particular section. This blind checkbox approach to development is dangerous. Information included in the course may not be relevant and—even worse—could be *completely* wrong. Not only might you spend double the effort combing through the final product to find mistakes, but you might actually miss one or two mistakes and critical, even safety-related items could be incorrect. If you are committed to making sure your work is quality output from the beginning, everyone wins in the end.

Is Organized

Organization is an essential aspect of a successful technical developer. You should be able to keep track of your working files and your correspondence with your SME. There is little that irritates SMEs more than to have to resubmit material or changes they already submitted once before, and there is little that is more frustrating for you than to be unable to locate a document that you knew was once in your possession. So do yourself a favor and have some sort of organizational system in place for your work process. What system you choose does not matter as much as just having *something* that works!

Uses Problem-Solving Skills

As a developer, you should be able to pull out problem-solving skills when an unexpected setback occurs. With technical training development, you must assume that setbacks are the norm. The potential for stumbling blocks is infinite, what with changes in product offerings, new best practices, equipment availability, standard practices, government regulations, and so on. You should be resourceful enough to be able to identify additional resources or solutions and capable enough to adapt to midcourse changes that need correction.

Is Able to Accept Unknowns

At times, the information an SME gives you will be so obscurely technical and so profoundly complicated that it would take you a decade to fully understand it. As such, sometimes you just need to take the information you are given and go with it, even if you don't completely understand it. Of course, to still have a quality product, you should verify that at least the *SME* understands what you have done and agrees with your documentation of a particular answer, but after you have verified this, sometimes, in the interest of your own sanity, you need to move on. You should strive for a quality product, but occasionally this means you will not understand every detail of the material and will just have to (hold your breath) trust your SME. Your SME, after all, has the final say on the technical content.

Is Dependable

Be where you say you will be and do what you say you will do. Nothing will kill your credibility more quickly than if you forget about a meeting with your SME or neglect to email or provide information you said you would. To be successful, be realistic about what you can do and then stick to that and only that.

Draws upon Knowledge of Adult Learning

Much of course development involves keeping in mind adult learners. As your role in the development team is to take into account adult learning principles and apply them to the technical material, it stands to reason you should be up-to-date on learning research.

Possesses Practical Experience in the Subject Area

Nothing can substitute for work experience in the industry in which you are creating training. For example, if you are writing about oil well drilling and you have actually worked as an oil driller for seven years, then that experience will be invaluable when creating a technical course. Any practical experience you can gain in your subject area is only going to help you when it comes time to start piling sentences together. If you don't already have the technical background, be open to other possibilities of learning information. You will be surprised at how much an SME will enjoy taking you out to the shop to show you how a tool is assembled or out to a job where you can see a service being performed. All of these practical experiences give you an edge when it comes time to start writing and developing. If you can understand even a piece of the topic, this can help you communicate better with your SME on the course.

Oh, and One More Thing: You Should Be Able to Write a Complete Sentence!

An extremely important tool a successful training developer should have is a strong writing ability. Your central role in the training process is to make the technical content as understandable as it can be. You need to be able to write and present your thoughts and words in a clear and concise format. The process of taking obscure technical jargon and putting it into an understandable format is, simply, your job.

As discussed, with technical training development, getting your job done means you are often dependent on your SME's expertise and information. Thus, the ability to communicate effectively and work alongside all types of people, personalities, and egos is extremely important.

Traits of the Ideal Subject Matter Expert

For technical training, there is one very important person whom you cannot afford to have miscast: your main SME. The ideal traits of an SME are described below.

Has Knowledge of the Subject

As the name implies, the SME should be an expert in the subject matter of the course. If the SME does not really know the content, you may have approximate or incorrect material in the course. An SME with good knowledge of the subject will be able to provide technical information that is useful and valuable.

Noted

SMEs without good knowledge of the subject may exhibit avoidance behaviors. Avoidance behaviors may initially leave you thinking that your SME simply does not care or does not have time for the project. But sometimes a problem SME who fails to follow through on tasks or answer questions simply does so because he or she does not fully understand the subject and is thus unable to do what you request, rather than *unwilling* to do it.

Utilizes Good Communication Skills

A major predictor of the success of a project is how well the SME communicates. As much of an SME's workflow involves explaining complicated content to a developer who might not understand a lot about the subject, the SME who can explain things simply and concisely not only makes life much easier for you but helps to ensure the success of the project.

Is Available

An SME should have enough time to devote to the project. Ideally, the SME should have a full-time focus (even if only temporarily) on the course development. This can end up being a challenge, because good SMEs usually have a lot of responsibilities because, simply, they are good at what they do. It does not matter how qualified your SME is or how well he or she communicates; if your SME does not have time in his or her schedule to help you, the project will not go well. SMEs with appropriate availability for your project will answer your emails and do things on time, both very important requirements for the success of the project.

Has Experience Designing a Course

Just as it is helpful for a developer to have practical experience with a technical subject, it is also helpful for an SME to have practical experience designing a course. This can save you time. You won't have to spend as much time explaining each step in the course design process if you are working with an SME who has put together a course before. In addition, if the SME has been through the course design process once before, he or she may be more willing to give you information. The SME might have a better idea of why you ask all those annoying questions, and he or she will probably trust that all the inconvenience is worth the good courseware produced in the process.

Possesses Knowledge of Adult Learning

People are not likely to invest in things they don't understand. If an SME does not understand adult learning, there is the possibility that the SME will not find much worth in the instructional elements you include in the course. An ideal SME understands that a quality training program must follow accepted adult learning tactics. That is, the content being developed must be focused not on the instructor, but more on the learners. If your SME understands that the learners are the target of the program, he or she will be more likely to come up with helpful activities and support the eventual structure of the interactive course.

Admits When He or She "Just Doesn't Know"

Although an SME is expected to be an expert on the subject, there will be times that he or she does not know the answer to a technical question. An ideal SME will be straightforward and admit this, and then either ask for more time to find the answer or give you the contact details of someone who may be better able to find it.

Is Connected

An effective SME should have numerous contacts and resources to share. The other technical people the SME has access to, along with the electronic or hard-copy resources the SME has available, allow you to avoid wasting time when gathering and developing material.

Is Neither Too General nor Too Detailed

For most situations, the SME should be neither too general nor too detailed. For example, if an SME provides information that is too general, it can be hard to make the class challenging. In addition, broad statements can leave room for too much interpretation and, thus, could lead to errors as materials are developed. Information that is too general can also cause misunderstandings as the learners try to make sense of the material. But having too many details can be a problem as well. Information-overload can overwhelm the learners. Also, being too detailed becomes a problem when it paralyzes a perfectionist SME and he or she is unable to continue on with the project because it is not absolutely perfect. Your SME should provide just the right amount of detail necessary to meet the course objectives.

Is Decisive

As the SME is in charge of the technical information included in the course, he or she must be able to make concrete decisions that solve issues regarding message and information. Indecisiveness will always prolong the project and frustrate the process. A decisive SME can focus your message and streamline the course.

Cares

A disillusioned SME who doesn't care for the company or the target audience probably won't be helpful on the course development project. On the flip side, an SME who truly cares about the organization and, more important, the target audience, is probably going to translate much of that goodwill into a quality work product for your training course.

In summary, a good SME is needed as both a guide and a resource throughout the project. The SME should have extensive experience with the topic and, when asked, should intimately understand what the areas of focus must be for the target audience.

Finding a Good SME

Now, the question you may be asking yourself is, *How do I find this person?* It is usually not hard to find a good SME if you focus on a few specific things. When considering a possible candidate, follow these steps:

> ▶ Ask a few questions about the technical topic and judge the quality of the response in terms of understandability, length, and voice tone (exasperated at the onset is not a good sign).
> ▶ Send out an introductory exploratory email and note the length of time it takes you to receive an answer. If an SME doesn't respond to your initial email for weeks, assume this will be the case for every question you ask throughout the project.

▶ Ask around. If you are familiar with other individuals in the organization, try to ask them about their experiences working with a particular person. You may find out that "this SME is a nightmare," or that "this SME is the best person ever."

▶ Determine whether your SME will be directly affected by the business impact your course will have. If your SME is also a stakeholder in the outcome of the project, you will probably have more luck.

Basic Rule

Try to get the names of at least three SMEs to contact. Subject matter experts are busy, and the more SMEs you can secure as *potential* contacts, the better off, ultimately, you are going to be.

What We've Learned

A course development project involves two different but equally important roles. On one side is the developer, who is responsible for course structure, organization, and learning theory. On the other side is the SME, who is responsible for the technical content within the course structure.

For a project to be completed efficiently and effectively, the SME and the developer must each possess a set of ideal characteristics related to their roles. Both roles are indispensable to course development. Without either one, the finished product will be insufficient.

Getting It Done

Being aware of your development team's strengths and weaknesses is your first step toward success. The following inventories are designed to get you and your SME thinking about how potential problem areas might be avoided. They will also provide an important first step in communication and will help your SME understand what is expected during the project.

Worksheet 2–1. Evaluate Your Skills

Complete the following assessment tool. Rate yourself from 1 to 5, with 1 the weakest and 5 the strongest, on each of the following characteristics. Then describe how you plan to improve or maintain each rating.

Developer Characteristic	Rating (1–5)	My Plans to Improve
Utilizes good people skills		
Doesn't give up easily		
Asks questions		
Is a good listener		
Applies knowledge of instructional design		
Draws upon a sense of humor		
Desires to understand a complicated topic		
Accepts criticism		
Is adaptable		
Requires a quality product		
Is organized		
Uses problem-solving skills		
Is able to accept unknowns		
Is dependable		
Draws upon knowledge of adult learning		
Possesses practical experience in the subject area		
Has good writing skills		

Worksheet 2–2. Evaluate the Skills of the SME

Explain the following characteristics to your SME. Ask him or her to fill out the chart below about himself or herself, using the same rating system of 1 to 5. Then, together, both of you should share the results of your evaluations with each other.

SME Characteristic	Rating (1–5)	My Plans to Improve
Has knowledge of the subject		
Utilizes good communication skills		
Is available		
Has experience designing a course		
Possesses knowledge of adult learning		
Admits when he or she doesn't know an answer		
Is connected		
Is neither too general nor too detailed		
Is decisive		
Cares		

3

Beginning the Technical Training Project

What's Inside This Chapter

In this chapter, you'll learn

▶ why an initial course design meeting is important, who should attend, and what should be accomplished
▶ important questions to ask
▶ what is in a course starter packet.

Communication is at the core of successful technical training projects. When a project gets started off with a healthy dose of communication, collaboration occurs and a better work product is likely to result. Conversely, without effective communication at the outset, the technical project may drag along, be fractured, or have something even worse occur. Consider the anecdote below:

Neil furrowed his brow as he studied a stack of papers placed on his desk. Just days ago, Neil was assigned to a technical training project for a biomedical research lab. Elyse, a biomedical research scientist, had created hundreds of PowerPoint slides of content she thought would be good for the course. Now Neil was tasked with taking this information and quickly "making a training class" out of it.

"Are you sure all this content belongs in this course?" Neil asked Elyse, who had just walked into his office.

"This is *all* important stuff," Elyse said impatiently as she tapped the papers.

"But is it absolutely necessary for lab technicians to know this information in order to correctly do their jobs?" Neil asked. "I don't know a lot about the topic yet, but from the type of information I'm seeing in this documentation, it looks as if it's geared more toward doctors than the technicians in the lab."

Elyse stared at him. "There is a chance we may have one or two doctors who decide they want to attend this course," she said.

"But isn't this course geared toward the lab technicians?" Neil asked.

"I am not following you. Who said that?" Elyse said.

Neil tried again. "Does this information from the last seven slides you gave me help in some way to meet the objectives of the course?"

Elyse studied Neil's face. "The point is that this information should be included in our class because we may have some people that don't know these things," she said. With that, she turned and started for the door.

"Besides," she called over her shoulder, "I'm not sure if you knew this, but all the equipment in the lab might be overhauled in another eight months, so 80 percent of the course content we have so far might end up being obsolete anyway."

Neil sighed. It really was going to be a long project.

■ ■ ■ ■ ■

Like Neil, some of us may have experienced technical training projects that did not get started well. Consider some of the issues from this scenario:

> ► **Needs Analysis:** The most obvious problem with the scenario above is that a good needs analysis was not completed before the training development started. Without a solid needs analysis, technical training development projects are doomed to fail.

> ► **Target Audience:** There was no clear target audience defined, and so Neil had no ground to stand on when he made the assumption that the target audience of the course was lab technicians.

▶ **Course Objectives:** It also appeared that no course objectives had been written down. Without anything defined, it was difficult for Neil to reason with Elyse as to whether material belonged in the course or not.

▶ **Relevancy of Information:** In addition, Neil had no idea that particular lab equipment was likely to become obsolete. Knowing which equipment was likely to go away could have helped him focus his time and energy on the correct and relevant information; perhaps this course wasn't even necessary to meet any real business needs of the organization!

Neil could have headed off most of these issues if he had insisted that the technical training project be started in a more comprehensive way. If he had asked the right questions and documented the answers in a solid and visible design document, he might have avoided many of the problems he faced.

The ideal venue in which to address all these issues and create the conditions for a successful technical training project is the *initial course design meeting.*

The initial course design meeting is a great opportunity to get a solid start on your technical training project. By taking full advantage of this meeting, you can avoid many of the pitfalls that plagued Neil in the scenario above.

Basic Rule

Every technical training development project should begin with a course design meeting.

The Initial Course Design Meeting

The initial course design meeting sets the stage for the technical project. This meeting is where the scope of the project is laid out between you and your subject matter expert (SME). It is where you find out the business need for the course; that is, it is where you verify that a course and its objectives are relevant and necessary to the organization.

Besides giving you an indication of the overall picture of the course, the initial meeting gives you clues about what kind of material you are dealing with and, more important, with whom you will be working to complete the project.

Who Should Attend?

In the most basic technical training project, there will be at least three parties: the technical training developer, the SME, and the "stakeholder," or the person requesting the course. (Note: The SME can often fulfill both the role of the SME and the role of the stakeholder.) At the very least, the developer and the SME must attend the initial course development meeting. The SME who attends this meeting should know the business reasons for the course, the technical content, and the target audience. The SME should also be aware of the typical knowledge, skills, and job process of the target audience. Most important, the SME must be able to speak on what information should or should not be included in the course. If the SME does not have all that information, more parties must be included in the meeting, such as the stakeholder or someone who does know the business reasons for the course and its target audience.

What Should Be Accomplished?

The initial course meeting should provide you with enough information so that you can begin to document your design plan and course structure (described in detail in the next chapter). The main point of the meeting is for all parties to understand and agree on the following for the project:

- ▶ overall business goal
- ▶ target audience
- ▶ course objectives
- ▶ major course topics.

Eventually, as a result of this meeting, you will create a *design document* that spells out the items listed above. The design document functions as a plan for the project and is what you and your SME can work from as a roadmap.

It should be mentioned that this initial meeting is also an opportunity to set the tone of the project and the working relationship.

Noted

The initial project meeting is absolutely the most important face-to-face meeting you will have during the design process. *Real communication among the participants in this meeting is critical, and that means you must educate, question, and listen. Projects can completely derail because the SME/project initiator does not understand the instructional designer's role in the development. Use a visual description of the process, explain what you do precisely, and begin an open discussion and analysis of the organizational training needs. Remember, use as many learning style techniques as possible at this initial meeting until you understand the best method for your SME. You will need it in the future!*

—Patty Murdock, Technical Training Manager,
Schlumberger, Houston, Texas

Important Questions to Ask

As mentioned previously, a good needs analysis is essential in order to create an effective fit-for-purpose technical training course. The following are some sample questions that you can ask during your initial course design meeting.

What is the business goal this course is supposed to meet?

This is the *most important* question within the needs analysis. Before understanding how you will complete your course, you must understand why you are doing the course in the first place. To be relevant and valuable, every training course must have a sound business purpose. This purpose will guide you and your SME as you complete every chapter and make choices for the course.

Noted

The business need for a training course could be growth in the market, expanded product offerings, new product launches, implementation issues, and so on. A lot of times people assume the business need is just "profit," when actually the business need is directed by something more complex.

—Kenny Amend, Area Manager,
Weatherford International, Houston, Texas

Who is the target audience? How is one identified as part of the target audience?

This question seems simple, but in these times of sprawling organizations with multifaceted employee populations, it is often difficult to answer. You will be surprised at how often an SME or even the stakeholder will have trouble pinpointing the target audience. Sometimes the target audience will be identified by a particular job title within a particular geographic location in a specific product line. Other times, it will be a combination of factors you never even considered. Regardless, the answer to this question cannot be put off, as it is instrumental in narrowing your focus and allowing you to understand your target audience's needs.

Do all members of the target audience belong to one job title?

It is important that you determine whether the course content will be geared to many different job titles or just one. Differing job titles will affect how you address the content. An audience that encompasses many job titles tends to be the case for foundational level courses or for courses focused on general tasks. If your target audience spans multiple job titles in the organization, you may need to be more general with your content, or you may need to make sure you draw in examples and data from lots of different areas of the organization so that the course is relevant to the entire target audience.

Do job descriptions exist for the target audience?

If you have formal documentation of job descriptions and competencies, these items will be extraordinarily valuable in helping you more accurately identify the needs of the target audience and the eventual course objectives.

This question will help you learn more about the background and existing knowledge of your target audience. With technical topics, varying skill levels will be present in an organization. Often, one of the chief complaints about a technical course is that the content does not match the target audience. If a course is too basic or too advanced for the target audience, the class is a waste of time. Understanding the skill level of the audience is critical in maximizing the benefit of the class.

Did the target audience receive a specific university degree or vocational certificate?

People who work in technical fields often must have associated university degrees or vocational certificates. You can research the qualifications and requirements of attaining a specific degree or vocation, and that knowledge will give you additional insight into your training topic. For example, you would speak to different areas of a topic if your audience was composed of doctors who have graduated from medical school, rather than lab technicians with a high school education.

Besides the primary target audience, is there a secondary audience that might attend the course?

Once you've established a primary target audience, it might sometimes be helpful to take into account a secondary audience as well. You will not specifically design the bulk of your content to suit your secondary audience, but you may find that you will throw in a note or two every so often in order to increase the footprint of your course. Accommodating the secondary audience of your training course, however, should not come at the expense of your target audience.

What are the SMART (Specific, Measurable, Achievable, Realistic, and Testable) objectives of this course?

Your attention to this single question should not be diminished. Your course objectives will guide every aspect of your course design and development, so it is imperative that you utilize SMART course objectives.

Where do this class and these objectives fit into the overall learning plan of the target audience?

Is this a beginning course, an intermediate course, or an advanced course? Knowing whether a course is fit for a beginning, intermediate, or advanced learner helps you determine what content to include and what level your material should reach. It can also give you a framework for how much of one topic to cover.

What is the work environment like for the target audience?

This question gets at the overall feel of a particular type of job. This is important to know, because besides giving you more insight into the characteristics of your target audience, knowing the typical job environment of your target audience can help you relate course content to the workplace and increase the credibility of the course. Understanding what a typical day is like for your target audience can help you determine what will work well in your course. If you have a bunch of rough and tough oil rig workers, for example, you may not want to start off your training class with everyone standing in a circle singing.

What resources do the target audience members already use on the job?

These may include computer programs, instruments, reference books, databases, data charts, and so on. This question is important because it can help you determine what you should include in your training materials. The question is also significant for another reason: If you are asking learners to complete an activity in class that replicates something they do on the job, you will want to keep in mind any job aids and resources they are likely to use on a daily basis. You probably will want to have these resources available during the course.

In the past, how has the target audience learned about this product or service? Are there any available materials already?

No matter how insignificant this question may seem, or how much pushback you get when you ask it, insist on an answer. A lot of informal training goes on in technical organizations. Before your training course existed, at least a few people somehow found a way to learn about the product or perform the task correctly. The answer to this question can give you clues about where to start your search for technical information.

Noted

Even if no information currently exists on your particular technical topic, you may still find it useful to determine how the target audience learned about other new (even unrelated) information. This can give you an insight into the typical knowledge pockets of an organization. The key is to identify potential locations of organizational resources.

Is this a new or an existing product or service?

This question can also give you insight into how difficult or easy it will be to secure information on your topic. If your course content covers a relatively new product or service, get ready to complete a lot of interviewing. If your course content covers an established product, prepare yourself for a lot of sifting and editing during the development process.

Does this product, service, or procedure change often?

Highly technical products or services often stay competitive by being on the cutting edge of technology. Unfortunately, this can pose some difficulties for training development. It can be a challenge keeping course materials current if a product is constantly changing. If you are not prepared for this at the beginning of a project, you may find it especially debilitating. Chapter 9 of this book, "Troubleshooting: Challenges and Solutions," discusses specific tactics for this type of situation.

What changes are likely to happen with this product, service, or procedure in the near future? In the distant future?

If the product or service is about to undergo a major overhaul, you will want to know. If management cannot yet articulate exactly what those specific changes will be, you should still try to get a basic idea of what may be coming in the future. You can help with the credibility, timeliness, and relevance of your course and your materials if you can demonstrate to learners that your training course is tied in to the future of the product or service.

Where does this product or task fit into the organizational scheme?

This question gives you an idea of the organization within which your target audience functions. Understanding how your course's product or task fits into the grand scheme of the organization can help you make connections with content and also identify potential sources of information.

How does the organization view this product or service?

This question warns you if you are stepping onto a land mine. You may be dealing with an unpopular topic or product; these types of hindrances can prevent a course from being successful. The best technical training projects can fail if there are organizational issues going against the topic or information. Your first line of defense is to understand these issues.

Where is the best place to start looking for resources internally?

SMEs should know the organization. That is, they are likely to have a good idea of where knowledge is stored and who knows what. This may seem simple, but you will be surprised at the gems you can find simply by asking SMEs where they find information. Ask. See what you can find out.

Has this topic or something similar ever been taught in the past?

This is another question designed to help you find hidden information. You will be surprised at how often you will be given a course request, only to find out that a similar course or learning solution existed in the past. Valuable information about products and services is often hidden away on computers in the form of customer presentations, job aids, or an entire host of other things.

Noted

If the SME is hesitant to give you "old" course material because it is outdated, explain that you wish to see it only to gain an understanding of one possible approach. Seeing an "old" version of a class can help you gain a further understanding of your topic, and at the very least, it could help prevent you from making the same mistakes that caused the course to become obsolete in the first place.

Noted

If there was a prior course, make sure it belongs to the organization. If the organization outsourced the original course, the materials might be copyrighted and not the property of the organization. Serious liability can occur if you and your SME inject material that was generated by a third party and that third party still owns the material.

Is there already a prerequisite course?

If so, request access to those materials. Prerequisite materials will give you an idea of the existing knowledge level of your target audience. A prerequisite course can also help educate you on your technical topic.

Is there a (different) finished training course that can be used as a model?

If so, ask to review that course to learn more about the stakeholder and SME's process and expectations. Seeing an example of a successful finished product that you can use as a formatting blueprint helps to ensure that you are meeting expectations of the company. A finished product can also give you an insight into current logos, styles, the "look" the company prefers, and so on.

Who are the experts?

You'll want to identify top performers of the service or those who are knowledge experts on the product. This question is important if your SME is not currently a member of the target audience. If your SME has not been a member of the target audience for a while, it is especially important that you gain the perspective of a top performer currently doing the job. This will help keep your content relevant. Top performers are often the closest to the topic and usually have good information stashed away on their computers, at their workstations, and in their minds. It is important that these current upstanding members of the target audience be identified and consulted to provide you with key information.

Who is the best internal source for additional information about this topic?

Try to get multiple names so you have backups to contact for information. Establishing early on that you will be utilizing various sources of information during development can prevent you from feeling later on in the project that you are in the middle of a turf war. Asking this question helps make it clear you are "approved to go to various sources for information," and that the course content won't just be based on one person's word. In addition, if for some reason your SME leaves the project, you still have other experts to whom you can turn.

What is the preferred method of contact regarding this project?

In order to work effectively with an SME, you must be able to communicate well with others. People have differing communication preferences. Some prefer email, while others choose to communicate face-to-face or by telephone. Understanding your SME's preference can help ease the communication process and get you the information you need to complete your course.

What external sources can go be called upon for additional information?

You might be surprised at the good sources of information your SME can point out. The web is a big place, but it can be made smaller if you know what to look for and some good key words to plug into search engines.

Who are the competitors of this product or service?

By researching competitors, you may find a valuable source of information. Although the competitors' products or services may be different, there must be similarities if they are considered to be competitors. Reading about how the competitors explain their products or services can help you gain a better understanding of the product or service your own course covers.

Are there any long lead-time items that need to be discussed?

Long-lead items include any needed equipment, models, animations, or graphics that do not yet exist. Often these items can be time-consuming or expensive to obtain and can involve people outside the immediate training department. You should do everything in your power to allow those other people time to accomplish what they need. Ideally, the development of the long-lead items should run concurrent with the course development.

Knowing whether you will be able to secure these long lead-time items will affect your course design. If you have models, simulations, graphics, or videos available, you will plan to build these into your course plan via exercises, discussions, practices, and so on. Ascertaining these longer lead-time items at the earliest stages of the project can save you time in the end.

How can the information attendees learn in the training course be supported once they are back on the job?

Subjects covered in a training class can be highly complicated and technical, so it makes sense to ask about how the course topic and materials can be supported once the target audience is back on the job. At the very least, asking this question gets your SME in the mindset of linking the training course to on-the-job performance.

How will the success of this course be determined?

This includes identifying what metrics and measures to use. This question helps to focus your design plan, and it again makes you and your SME specifically consider the business need of your course.

At the end of the project, you want to be able to supply data that quantifies the return on the investment of time, energy, and resources spent. Determining final measurements at the beginning of the project can help accomplish this.

Is there anything else that should be included?

Because often you don't know what you don't know about your technical topic, asking your SME whether you missed any important questions at the end of your meeting is good practice. Almost always, SMEs will add some important tidbit or mention an especially important point on which you should focus.

Asking the right questions at the beginning of a technical training project can get you headed toward success. The questions mentioned in this section are intended to give you a flavor of what you should ask during your needs analysis. Based on your topic and the answers you get from your SME, you will probably have to prepare follow-up questions to complete your analysis.

Basic Rule

Ask the right questions in your initial course design meeting.

Course Starter Packet

This chapter has discussed what information to collect during a face-to-face meeting with an SME. However, you can gather some information before this meeting, and you may consider creating a course starter packet to jump-start your development.

A course starter packet is a series of papers, forms, or references you give to an interested party who wishes to have a course or program developed. This packet is not intended to replace the face-to-face initial course design meeting; rather, it is intended to enhance that get-together. As your SME reads and fills out this paper-work, he or she should start to get into an ideal frame of mind for the initial course design meeting.

The following are general sections of a course starter packet.

1. What's in It for the SME?

As for anything else, your SME needs sufficient motivation to have his or her course developed. You need to explain why having you design or redesign a course is a good idea. At the very beginning, include a short paragraph on the benefits of the design process to the organization. You must truly sell the benefits of the project here. If you can get your SME to begin with the end in mind, you will more easily be able to convince your SME that you have shared goals, and the entire process will go more smoothly.

Noted

Keep the packet as short as possible. You don't want to overburden your SME with too much at once. Include only the most important points you intend to cover or emphasize in your initial course design meeting. Keep it simple.

2. What to Expect
   a. General process
   b. Expectations

Being up-front about the process helps to place everyone's expectations in the same arena. You should explain briefly the general phases of the process. Be clear about the things you want. For example, if you would like to check in with your SME once per week, ask for this.

3. Introductory Questions
   a. Contact information
   b. Business need of the course
   c. Typical audience
   d. How the course will be measured
   e. Course objectives
   f. Resources available

As discussed previously, you will want to ask a variety of questions related to your course content. These introductory questions will help get your SME to begin thinking about these issues so he or she develops a better mindset before you begin. They will also help you to gather some basic information.

4. Principles of Adult Learning
   a. Characteristics of adult learners
   b. Additional resources

Many people, especially in the technical industries, assume that lecture equals training. Start debunking this myth early by showing examples of educational research on the effectiveness of different teaching methods. Consider including additional links or a bibliography of works available on adult learning or instructional design. Encourage your SME to look these over. Remember, the more your SME knows about what you are doing, including all the benefits, the more he or she is likely to buy into the process and make your job easier and more successful.

Getting It Done

This chapter marks the formal start of the course development process. You can avoid the pitfalls mentioned in the scenario at the beginning of the chapter if you are prepared and begin your technical project with a comprehensive course design meeting with your SME. The initial course design meeting sets the stage for the technical project. You should ask the right questions in order to determine the overall business goal, your target audience, the course objectives, and the major course topics. You can prepare your SME for these questions by creating paperwork (in the form of a course starter packet) that he or she can fill out before your initial course design meeting.

Launching your technical training project in a comprehensive way helps ensure that you are meeting the business goals of your organization and addressing the needs of your target audience.

Worksheet 3–1. Initial Course Design Meeting

The following is a worksheet you can use to prepare for your initial course design meeting.

1. Who needs to attend my initial course design meeting?

2. What questions do I need to ask during the initial course design meeting?

Worksheet 3–2. Course Starter Packet

The following is a worksheet you can use to prepare your own course starter packet to give to your SME. Please note that you will need to attach the specific adult learning sources you would like to discuss with your particular audience.

Valuable Training

The instructional development process you will be part of helps to implement training that tackles our organization's needs by specifically structuring content that intentionally targets individual learning and retention.

Creating a course involves

- identifying the business purpose, the target audience, and the objectives of the course
- planning and developing the instructional strategies to teach the needed information and skills
- implementing and evaluating the course.

Please remember to keep an open mind, give input, and stick to deadlines during the process.

Please fill out the following information.

Name: _____ Email: _____

What is the business need for this course?

Who is the target audience of this course?

How will we measure the success of this course?

What are the SMART (Specific, Measurable, Achievable, Realistic, and Testable) objectives of this course?

What technical resources are available?

Thank you for your help in this project!
For more information, please email me at_____.

4

Arranging a
Technical Course

What's Inside This Chapter

In this chapter, you'll learn

▶ the building blocks of a course design document, including an appropriate and complete topical outline
▶ various options for organizing a technical course, along with the benefits and drawbacks of each style.

Now that you have asked the questions appropriate for determining the audience, business purpose, and objectives of your course, it is time to compile these items into a solid design document.

The course design document is your roadmap for the entire course development process. The design document is your means to determine exactly what the course will be. This chapter covers the intricacies involved in creating a complete and accurate design document. It also covers options for organizing your material so that the course objectives are supported as much as possible.

The Building Blocks of a Course Design Document

Creating your course design document is one of the most important tasks you will complete for your technical course development project. The design document is where you determine specifics of what the course will cover. At a minimum, your design document should contain

- ▶ a working title for the project
- ▶ the agreed-on audience
- ▶ SMART (Specific, Measurable, Achievable, Realistic, and Testable) course objectives
- ▶ a topical outline.

Basic Rule

Your course design document should contain your title, audience, objectives, and course topics.

In your course design document, you may also include animations, graphics, models, or other items that have long lead times to produce, as well as a list of available resources, a list of prerequisite courses, and a description of accompanying job aids.

The Topical Outline

The largest section contained within your course design document is your topical outline. The topical outline is a detailed outline of each concept to be covered during the course. Every technical item on the outline needs to relate back to one of the SMART course objectives (see Figure 4–1). You will probably find that the topical outline is the most challenging part of the design document to create.

Noted

If you are working with a subject matter expert (SME) who has never helped create a course design document, it may help to show him or her an example of a design document from another course or the document in this book so that both of you are operating from the same frame of reference.

Figure 4–1. Sample Course Design Document

Principles of POS Software

Audience

POS technicians with 2 to 3 months' experience in the lab

Prerequisites

Basic POS terminology

SMART Course Objectives

At the end of this course, learners should be able to

- navigate successfully around the POS system
- create a field report
- adjust the inputs of the sales report to create a usable field report and explain the rationale behind these decisions.

Topical Outline

- Course introduction
  - ▶ Safety
  - ▶ Learner introductions
  - ▶ How to get the most out of this course
- Navigating the software
  - ▶ Hydraulic Data Tab
  - ▶ Job Input Tab
  - ▶ Verification Tab
  - ▶ Exercise: Software Scavenger Hunt
    - Learners will open up a preloaded job file and find answers to various questions (e.g., What is the hydrostatic pressure of product #2, according to this job data?).
- Creating an analysis
  - ▶ Basic information
  - ▶ Applications
  - ▶ Exercise: Information Needed
    - Before covering the type of information needed to create a field report, learners will have to brainstorm what information is needed. They should be divided into groups, with each group reporting their findings on a flip chart.
  - ▶ Job information form
    - Customer data
    - Mechanical, Hydraulic, and Chemical Principles
  - ▶ Exercise: Signore Enterprises Job Order—Part A
    - Learners will be given raw job data to input into the system to create a preliminary output.

Continued

Figure 4–1. Continued

- Contingencies
  - ▶ Planning for the unexpected
  - ▶ Common errors
  - ▶ Adjusting for new regulations
  - ▶ Exercise: Signore Enterprises Job Order—Part B
    - Learners will be given additional information about the job that they previously entered into the POS system. Based on this information, they will make adjustments to the various fields in each of the software tabs and print out an adjusted, usable report. Learners should be able to explain the rationale behind their choices.
  - ▶ Exercise: Course Reflection
    - Learners will write down three things they learned during the course and how they will apply this information to their jobs.

As you create your design document, you need to be sure that the outline is complete and that it takes into account parallel and unparallel concepts. These items will be discussed below.

Completeness of Outline

You should be aware of whether particular sections in your outline are complete or incomplete. You can determine whether a section is complete by referring to the course objectives. All of the objectives should be met through the course topics represented. If the course objectives are not met by the items listed, you have an incomplete section.

Consider the objectives from the previous outline, shown in Figure 4–2.

Figure 4–2. Course Objectives from the Course Design Document

Course Objectives

At the end of this course, learners should be able to
- navigate successfully around the POS system
- create a field report
- adjust the inputs of the sales report to create a usable field report and explain the rationale behind these decisions.

This time, however, imagine that as you put together the topical outline, you find that your coverage of topics is skewed. In this instance, the topic is heavy on data for "Navigating the software" and quite sparse for "Creating an analysis" and "Contingencies." This outline demonstrates the way in which technical developers many times receive material. It is up to you to recognize when an outline is skewed and does not contain complete information (see Figure 4–3).

Figure 4–3. Sample Topical Outline

Topical Outline
- Course introduction
  - ▶ Safety
  - ▶ Learner introductions
  - ▶ How to get the most out of this course
- Navigating the software
  - ▶ Hydraulic Data Tab
  - ▶ Job Input Tab
  - ▶ Verification Tab
  - ▶ Exercise: Software Scavenger Hunt
    - Learners will open up a preloaded job file and find answers to various questions (e.g., What is the hydrostatic pressure of product #2, according to this job data?).
- Creating an analysis
  - ▶ ????
- Contingencies
  - ▶ ????

Parallel and Unparallel Concepts Taken into Account
You should also be aware of the level of detail of particular topics on your outline. For example, let's say your technical course was about "Baking a Cake" and you had the topic list shown in Figure 4–4. The items in this outline are not all parallel concepts. "Measure correct amount of baking soda" is more detailed than the rest of the items in the outline. As such, you would want the outline to reflect this and would move "Measure correct amount of baking soda" to a subtopic in the appropriate place in the outline, as in Figure 4–5.

Figure 4–4. Unparallel Topics (Incorrect)

Baking a Cake
- Gather ingredients
- Measure correct amount of baking soda
- Mix ingredients
- Bake ingredients

Figure 4–5. Unparallel Topics (Corrected)

Baking a Cake
- Gather ingredients
  - ▶ Measure correct amount of baking soda
- Mix ingredients
- Bake ingredients

This may seem trivial, but as you move to more complicated topics it becomes even more important. Consider the example in Figure 4–6. If you are a nontechnical developer, you will not always understand the intricacies of your technical topic. But there are ways you can learn to think about technical subjects in order to create an appropriate and complete topical outline.

As you build a topical outline for a technical training class, you should be on the lookout for the following types of information:

- ▶ categories
- ▶ levels of information
- ▶ definitions
- ▶ components
- ▶ relationships
- ▶ analogies
- ▶ processes.

Keeping in mind what type of information you are gathering, as you compile it, will be important when you start to put together your outline and your course.

As you talk about technical information with your subject matter experts (SMEs), you should keep a finger on the category under which the information you are speaking

Figure 4–6. Unorganized Versus Organized Topic Lists

Unorganized Topic List	Organized Topic List

• Mirroring (mirror neuron system)
• Single unit recording
• Aggregate fields
• Mismatch negativity
• Parts of the brain
• Cognitive neuropsychology
• Cerebral cortex
• Broca's area
• Brain responses
• SPECT
• Change blindness
• Methods
• Psychophysics
	Parts of the brain
	  • Aggregate fields
	  • Cerebral cortex
	  • Broca's area
	Brain responses
	  • Mismatch negativity
	  • Mirroring
	  • Change blindness
	Methods
	  • Psychophysics
	  • Cognitive neuropsychology
	  • SPECT
	  • Single unit recording

about might fall, the level of information you are discussing (for example, whether it is a broad, abstract principle or a very small detail), whether the information is a definition or a component of a bigger piece, or whether two or more items are related.

Keep track of statements like this one: "The center component of Product A is pretty distinct compared to what was previously available with Product B." You may not understand just what the difference is between Product A and Product B, but you should be able to tell—based on how the two terms are discussed—that they should be in different categories. Sometimes you are not just listening for an understanding of the concept; you are also listening for key words that will clue you in to where this information is supposed to be organized. Keeping in mind the type of information you are talking about, as you are talking about it, can help you as you create your topical outline.

Basic Rule
You must be aware of what type of information you are dealing with as you develop your topical outline.

As you create the outline, be sure its organization makes logical sense. The next section discusses various options for arranging technical courses.

Noted

Nontechnical designers working with an SME may sometimes find that the course design document evolves as the project evolves. It is important to remember that just as you are learning about the technical topic, your SME is also probably facing a learning curve with all that goes into the course development process. Sometimes the SME won't realize until further into the development process that the level of information is skewed or that a necessary topic has been omitted from the course. Of course, you should still ask the appropriate "why this change now" question to ensure that you are not dealing with scope creep, but ultimately you need to be open and somewhat flexible with the design document as the course progresses.

Options for Arranging a Technical Course

A developer should always have a big picture of the chosen organizational system of the course in mind as he or she gathers information. Keeping this in mind will help you recognize where in the course to place any spontaneous technical tidbits you might catch, as well as alert you to when you might even need to change the course structure as the project evolves.

Noted

It is not uncommon for the course structure to change—sometimes several times during the design process. As you learn more about the topic and understand the level of detail with which the SME is working, you might realize that a more logical order of the course is appropriate.

The following sections describe various options for arranging technical training courses.

Organization by Order of Job Process

A course can be organized in the order in which tasks are completed in the target audience's job. A course organized in this way may have three sections:

1. Pre-job or task preparation

2. Tasks done during the job

3. Post-job procedures

If there are specific products covered, those products would be covered in turn in each section of the course, as in the example in Figure 4–7. This type of organization is ideal for training courses tailored to a very specific target audience in which all members hold the same job title.

Figure 4–7. Order in the Job Process

Overview

Pre-job
Product 1
Product 2
Product 3

Job
Product 1
Product 2
Product 3

Post-job
Product 1
Product 2
Product 3

Conclusion

Benefits: This type of course organization allows for instruction that is very close and relevant to the exact job of the target audience.

Drawbacks: Jumping around to different products during each section of the course (pre-job, job, and post-job) may be confusing to learners and make it difficult for them to remember what characteristics go with each product.

Organization by Product or Service

A course can also be organized based on the various products or services offered. The processes associated with each product or task (service) are covered completely in separate sections, as in Figure 4–8. This type of organization is ideal for training courses that cover distinct and individual products or tasks.

Figure 4–8. Organization by Products or Services

Overview		
Product/Task 1	**Product/Task 2**	**Product/Task 3**
Pre-job	Pre-job	Pre-job
Job	Job	Job
Post-job	Post-job	Post-job
Conclusion		

Benefits: This type of organization allows learners an opportunity to see how each product or service is specifically used in context.

Drawbacks: If a course is organized this way, there can be repetition of information covered about each product. Sometimes even very different products will have similar operational procedures.

Organization by Case Study

This type of course is organized around a case scenario. In this type of organization, learners are given a case study to complete. The steps they must follow function as the order of the course. Sometimes this type of course organization can look very similar to the order of the job process course organization system.

This type of organization is ideal when you have a comprehensive case study available that matches the objectives of the course. The case study structure gives learners a big picture of the situation, the topic, and the class and then allows them to go into detail from there. The case study organization works well for learners who desire to see the big picture before discussing details. It can also work well in courses in which participant discussion and extrapolation are required.

Benefits: The case study organizational style is usually quite engaging to the learners and relevant to their jobs, so organizing a course in this way can motivate them and help them directly relate training content to the workplace.

Drawbacks: This type of training can be quite time-consuming to develop. Also, not every topic fits nicely into a case study format.

Organization by Concepts: From Easy to Difficult

A course can also be organized by concepts—in this case, basic to complex (see Figure 4–9). Simple topics are covered first, and then these simple topics are used as building blocks for later, more complex topics. This type of organization is ideal when you have related topics that build on each other.

Figure 4–9. Organization by Concepts: Building from Easy to Difficult

This type of organization is also useful if most of your target audience is new to the field and unconfident; this structure gives a novice audience an easy win at the beginning of the class by providing "successes" with the easier topics at the beginning.

Benefits: This organizational structure allows learners to gradually and continually be challenged. Learners start with a relatively easy topic and are then allowed to build and apply that information to more difficult topics. Starting with an easier topic gives participants an early win in the training.

Drawbacks: This structure may not work for task-focused training. By organizing a course this way, you may be teaching participants concepts that are not consistent with the regular flow of their jobs. Task-based training should mirror the workplace as closely as possible, and this type of organizational structure may make that difficult to accomplish.

Organization by Concepts: Difficult, Then Build from Easy to Difficult

A course can also be organized by starting with a difficult topic, then moving back to an easy topic, and then building up in difficulty from there, as in Figure 4–10. This structure is useful if your target audience members are experienced individuals who don't necessarily think they need to be in training; this structure can provide a challenge right away in the course to pique the interest of more experienced learners.

Figure 4–10. Organization by Concepts: Difficult, Then Build from Easy to Difficult

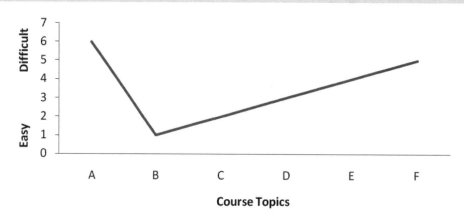

Benefits: Starting off with a difficult topic can spark interest and motivate learners to pay attention.

Drawbacks: This organizational structure may not follow the tasks of the job exactly. Also, if you misread your target audience and start out with something too difficult, they may never recover.

Organization by Concepts: Constant Variation Between Easy and Difficult

A course can also be organized by a back-and-forth combination of easy and difficult topics, as in Figure 4–11. The course may start with an easy topic, move to a difficult topic, then go back to an easy topic, return to a difficult topic, and so on.

Figure 4–11. Organization by Concepts: Easy, Difficult, Easy, Difficult

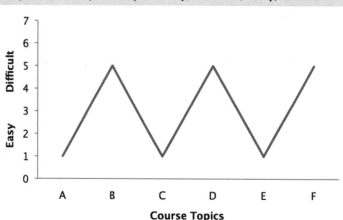

Figure 4–12. Organization by Concepts: Difficult, Easy, Difficult, Easy

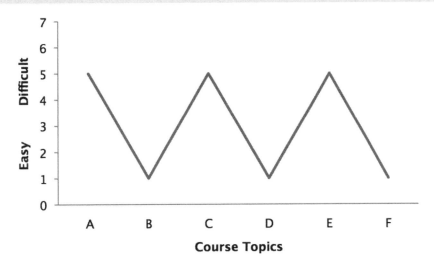

Conversely, a course can also be organized by starting with a *difficult* topic, then moving to an easy topic, then going back to a difficult topic, returning to an easy topic, and so on (see Figure 4–12).

A further application of this concept is to vary the easy and difficult concepts, but to maintain a slight upward (toward difficult) progression as you go through the class (see Figure 4–13). This provides much-needed breaks, but also a more likely chance that learners won't struggle as much with the difficult topics because the appropriate building blocks will be in place.

Figure 4–13. Organization by Concepts: Building Easy, Difficult, Easy, Difficult

These organizational structures can be useful when training topics are variable in their difficulty, or for classes that have very complicated material that is likely to make learners "burn out." Having the easy-difficult or difficult-easy interchange gives learners much-needed breaks during the course.

Benefits: This structure allows learners breaks in the difficulty of training. Participants are kept challenged, but not completely burned out.

Drawbacks: This organizational structure may not follow the tasks of the job exactly. Also, if you misread your target audience and have an overly basic section at the beginning with experienced learners, those participants might be bored and have a bad first impression of the class. On the other hand, if you have an overly complicated section at the beginning with novice learners, the topic may go completely over their heads.

Learner Choice

It may sound frightening, but another option is to allow learners to choose what topics are covered and in what order. This type of organization is ideal when you have motivated participants ready to take charge of their learning. It is good for learners who have reached the "conscious incompetence" stage of being, that is, for those who are aware of what they don't know about a particular topic.

Noted

If learners are choosing their own topics, you will have to indicate this in the wording of the course objectives.

If it is not appropriate to let learners have control over all of the topics covered in training, you may consider simply allowing them to determine the order in which topics are covered. If you have topics of parallel importance and levels of complication (see Figure 4–14), letting learners choose the order in which those topics are covered will give them at least *some* tangible control over their learning.

Benefits: The benefit of this structure is that learners have control of their learning. This can motivate participants to be actively engaged.

Drawbacks: This structure may not work for learners who are still at the unconscious incompetence stage of learning, as they won't even know what topics they should be asking for in order to improve their performance. In addition, with this type of structure, your control over the organization of the course is lost. The course

Figure 4–14. Learner Choice

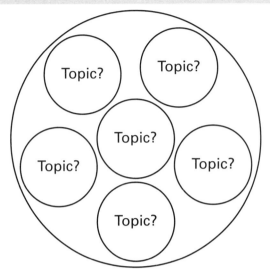

flow may not be efficient. There could be a repeat of topics that, had you organized the course a particular way, you could have consolidated. You may lose a logical flow—a related product or service that builds on another may not be covered right after the other. You may also run the risk of starting off with a topic that is too difficult and having to explain the easier building blocks within that difficult topic, thus not really allowing learners to choose the order of the topics and just generally confusing everyone.

Combination

Because not everything fits nicely into a category, you may find you need to use a combination of different organizational structures to fit your particular case. The *combination* organizational structure may be just the right fit for a number of tricky classes that don't seem to fit perfectly into another category.

The combination organizational structure can look like many different things; the three images in Figure 4–15 are simply examples. For example, in Combination 1, each product is discussed separately according to that product's distinct pre-job planning and job operations. Since all the products share basically the same post-job procedures in this case, the post-job procedures of all the products are discussed together. In Combination 2, all of the products have similar pre-job procedures, but have distinctly different job and post-job operations. Thus the pre-job procedures are covered together and the job and post-job operations are covered separately per

Figure 4–15. Combination

Example of Combination 1

Overview		
Product 1 Pre-job Job	**Product 2** Pre-job Job	**Product 3** Pre-job Job
Post-job Product 1 Product 2 Product 3		
Conclusion		

Example of Combination 2

Overview		
Pre-job Product 1 Product 2 Product 3		
Product 1 Job Post-job	**Product 2** Job Post-job	**Product 3** Job Post-job
Conclusion		

product. Finally, in Combination 3, all pre-job planning procedures are covered together. Then participants are allowed to choose the order of which of the three products they would like to cover.

Benefits: The combination course structure allows you the flexibility to fit an ideal organizational structure to your unique technical topic.

Drawbacks: If the organization gets too patchy or decentralized, your course structure is at risk of losing its organizational logic and can result in a completely *unorganized* flow. You need to keep this in mind if you start to mix together too many organizational structures.

Figure 4–15. Combination

Example of Combination 3

Overview

Pre-job
Product 1
Product 2
Product 3

Job Product

Job Product   Job Product

Learner Choice

Product 1	Product 2	Product 3
Job	Job	Job
Post-job	Post-job	Post-job

Conclusion

Getting It Done

After you have gathered all the necessary information (audience, business purpose, and objectives) for your technical course development project, the next step is compiling, analyzing, and arranging this information. This chapter has discussed creating a design document that fully supports the course objectives and the overall business goal. It is necessary to identify all of the topics necessary for a course and to determine the order in which those topics should be arranged.

There are many ways in which a course can be organized, each with its own benefits and drawbacks. You will need to look at your specific topic and course objectives in order to determine which structure is ideal.

Worksheet 4–1. Course Design Document Checklist

Use the following checklist to ensure that you have a complete and accurate course design document.

My outline has the following:

- ✓ Working title
- ✓ Audience
- ✓ Business purpose
- ✓ SMART objectives
- ✓ Topic list
- ✓ Complete content: All relevant content to meet course objectives is included.
- ✓ Appropriate categories and levels of information: Content is staged correctly on the outline.
- ✓ A logical flow: Course topics flow in a manner conducive to the target audience and the course objectives.

Worksheet 4–2. Choosing a Course Structure

Answering the following questions will help you choose an appropriate organizational structure for your technical training project.

1. Is this training topic about a product or a task?

2. How similar are the various products or tasks I am covering in my training? How much of the content is likely to overlap?

3. What are my target audience members like? Are they likely to appreciate a challenge at the beginning of the course, or would a challenge intimidate them or hamper their learning?

4. How motivated are the target audience members?

5. If participants chose their own order of topics covered, would the training be adversely affected? Would time be wasted?

5

Gathering Information

 What's Inside This Chapter

In this chapter, you'll learn

- ▶ types of information to seek
- ▶ in-house sources of information
- ▶ external sources of information
- ▶ how to maximize information you receive
- ▶ how to organize your information
- ▶ challenges and solutions associated with gathering technical data.

Gathering information for your technical training project can be the largest challenge you face during development. It is important that you understand what type of information you are seeking. You need to be able to dig into as many internal and external sources of information as you can find. When you do find a source of information, you should attempt to maximize the amount of material you attain and organize it in a logical manner. There are multiple challenges to gathering information, but every challenge can be met if you keep a persistent attitude.

Types of Information to Seek

As you gather information for a technical training class, there are certain types of information that you should seek:

- ▶ categories
- ▶ levels of information
- ▶ definitions
- ▶ components
- ▶ relationships
- ▶ analogies
- ▶ processes.

In general, you should first catalogue information you have, thinking about it in terms of the types of information listed above. Then, based on this assessment, you should seek information that fills the gaps. To complete your technical class, you are likely looking for one or more of the following: facts, case examples, diagrams, definitions, processes, procedures, best practices, contingencies, components, descriptions of internal functioning, typical errors, calculations, paperwork, charts, graphs, equations, scientific principles, troubleshooting or decision trees, applications, limitations, features, benefits, systems, job conditions, guidelines, rules of thumb, maintenance procedures, service procedures, assembly instructions, disassembly instructions, checklists, accessories, available upgrades, toolface or equipment readings, pre- and post-job checks, operational steps or events, functions, safety issues, menus, diagrams, models, and illustrations.

In-house Sources of Information

Every organization has information that will be found (or hidden) in different locations. There is no consistent place to look. You will need to analyze the organization you are working with and think about where you might search and who is likely to have access to the information you need.

When considering in-house sources of information, you might try these approaches:

Ask other SMEs. It can be helpful to gain additional perspectives on a source you have attained. After you have soaked up all that one subject matter expert (SME) has to say about a particular source, you can talk to other SMEs to see if they can offer additional insights. Often, you may find key words and phrases spur different information depending on the background of that particular SME. This means of gathering information is key when no written formal procedures are present and (somewhat informal) best practices are all that exist.

Ask someone within your target audience. This tactic has similar benefits to the "ask other SMEs" approach, but it provides a different perspective. Asking someone who does the job day in and day out what he or she thinks about a particular source or technical topic can give you incalculable benefits and insights.

Study old job reports. Often, old job reports and job paperwork are treasure troves of information. They often may fairly easily be turned into case studies, and the wording that job reports use can clue you in on the correct way to approach a technical topic.

The following are additional examples of internal sources of information:

- intranet site
- R&D/engineering department records
- local IT server
- HR department records
- old training manuals
- operation/service manuals
- marketing brochures and presentations
- IT document library
- job aids around the workplace (formal or informal)
- work orders.

Of course, you can always ask the IT manager, HR representatives, technical writers, R&D/engineering supervisors, secretaries, technicians, or programmers, among others, for additional information.

Think About This

Sometimes the information you need exists, but you are simply not asking questions that will help you attain it. The following questions can help lead you to internal sources of information.

• Who is likely to know about this process?

• Does any documentation already exist for this product or service (task)?

• How did employees find information about this product or service in the past? Did any documentation exist? What kind of instruction did they receive? Were they given a presentation?

• In general, how do employees find answers to their technical questions? If employees have a question about how this product or service works, where or to whom do they go?

• Is there a person who would have access to old job reports?

• Do you have any information on your computer or in your office that might be helpful for someone new to the job?

• What kinds of cheat sheets or references do people use to help them do their jobs?

• What information do you wish you had when you started in this position?

• Is there a location where information is saved—a file cabinet, a server, a SharePoint site, anything?

• Can I see the work space of a few members of our target audience?

• What information is produced when a job is completed?

Often, developing technical training courses is like going on a scavenger hunt for information. You will be surprised by the leaps and gains you can make simply by asking a variety of questions!

Basic Rule
Questions about *where* to find information are valid and good questions to pose during the development process.

Your best bet is to find information internally; however, there are instances when it can be very helpful—and necessary—to turn to external sources of information.

External Sources of Information

Outside sources of information vary from industry to industry. However, if you know where to look, you can often find useful data related to your course objectives from sources of information outside of your organization. The following are some examples of outside sources of information.

Blogs and Forums

Internet communities and discussion boards can give you great insight into the typical job issues of your target audience. Blogs and forums can be an unequaled source of informal information—especially if your technical topic is somewhat obscure and not likely to be represented in major websites.

Wikipedia

Wikipedia, an online encyclopedia, is typically a more vetted source of informal information than most blogs. Still, Wikipedia is an Internet source with fluctuating editors, so information gained from the site should be treated accordingly.

Books

This may seem obvious, but books in general still remain credible, vetted sources of information.

Academic Journal Articles

Academic journal articles can give you great perspective on the topic. Often these will clue you in to a specific portion of your technical topic. Sometimes using academic journal articles involves sifting through a lot of information, but if you are able to do this and you have the ability to summarize well, the payoff can be great.

Universities (Professors, Departmental Websites, Listserves, and So On)

Academia is a great source of information. Often you can contact a department and find professors who have some insight on your technical topic and would be more than happy to share it with you as long as you properly cite them.

Competitor Websites

While competitors' products are not the exact same products as those of your organization, if a competitor is truly a competitor, there must be some similarities in your product offerings. The mention of competitor websites does not advocate illegal corporate espionage, but rather refers to information that is freely available on the competition's website or in product sales brochures. Seeing how a competitor explains a product can help you understand and describe your own product better.

Government Websites

The governments of various countries host a variety of informational, credible websites on a variety of topics.

Safety Accreditation Organizations

Safety is a driving force in most technical industries. As such, external safety organizations often have information available that can translate into material that helps to meet your course objectives.

Industry Professional Organizations

Related professional organizations frequently have valuable resources available on their websites. These professional organizations also tend to hold training courses and sponsor conferences—both of which are places where you would have the opportunity to learn about your technical topic.

Noted

You will need to *internally* verify any information you receive from an external source, regardless of how valid that source may appear.

Maximizing Information You Receive

As we all know, technical information is often difficult to attain. As such, it is important that you optimize the technical information you *do* receive. The following are tactics for making the most out of material coming to you.

Double-check with Your SME Before You Eliminate Information

Before you decide to trash a source, ask your SME if the material is something that could be used in any other particular place in the course.

Don't Automatically Discount Sources

If you are not familiar with your technical topic, you should keep in mind, as you try to make sense of the information coming to you, that you are still a relative novice on the topic. With this said, don't automatically discount sources you don't understand. Sometimes a particular piece of information requires other information to be fully understood. You will likely not understand every little thing the SME wants to incorporate into the class. You don't want to limit the course material based on your own understanding of the content. Sometimes, even though you don't understand it, a particular topic will have to be included or dropped just because the SME "says so."

Noted

Your SME should be able to rationalize to you why information needs to be included or dropped, but if you don't understand the explanation, you may just have to go on faith that the SME knows something from all his or her years of experience that you don't fully understand yet. As long as your SME provides a rationale that seems reasonable, move on and accept that you aren't likely to understand every single word, phrase, or topic included in the class.

Save Emails

You never know when what has been said previously about a topic will suddenly make sense to you. Periodically during the project (especially if you hit a rough patch), revisit old emails to see if you can glean any additional content.

Read It Twice

If written material is highly technical, it may take you a couple of times reading through it to begin to understand everything the source has to offer.

Save It for Later

Don't throw away any of your sources. Log them and put them in a safe place, whether they are hard copies or electronic sources. After you have learned more about your topic, you may find it helpful to revisit those sources you read during your early days of learning about the topic. As you will by then have additional knowledge, the initial sources you analyzed may make more sense, answer outstanding content questions, and contain valuable information that should be included in the material!

Organizing Your Information

Part of gathering information involves organizing the information you receive. You can possess the best information in the world, but if you are not able to access it, the information does you no good. Also, little will ruin your credibility more than having to ask an SME for a document that he or she has already given you once before.

As you receive information, you will need to create an organizational system with the following characteristics:

- ▶ It allows you to store information.
- ▶ It allows you to easily *find* information. That is, the organizational system is convenient to your work flow and indexes data in some way.
- ▶ The system will still make sense to you if you end up stepping away from the project for a while or if the project gets put on hold for a few months.
- ▶ It communicates what you already have. With so many files in and out, it can be a challenge to see clearly what data you currently possess. Sometimes a document listing sources with a brief description of their content and purpose (that is, an annotated bibliography) can save you time for large projects, projects extended over a period of time, and projects that include many different levels of courses (with different developers). Also, it will ensure that you don't have to ask an SME for a document that he or she has already given you once before.

The specific organizational system you have is not as important as simply the fact that you have a system. Your organizational system can take a variety of forms.

Essentially, as you collect materials, you are matching content gathered with your topical outline and objectives and placing these materials within the section they are most likely to represent.

You might, for example, take an empty three-ring binder with each tab representing a different topic, chapter, or section of the course; you may then index all of the materials you receive under these tabs. You can also accomplish this electronically with a file folder system with electronic documents placed within each folder. Cloud-based software, where data is stored on the Internet and can be accessed globally, is another option for tracking and organizing data.

Noted

I've found that gathering material for a new technical writing project can be overwhelming without organization. Digital materials provided by my SMEs, supporting resources located through other contacts, and articles and clippings from professional journals accumulate rapidly. To stay on top of the volume, I create a set of virtual folders with descriptive labels where I store the resources for each topic and subtopic. That way, when I am ready to write, everything I need is in one place and I don't lose time searching for lost items.

—Stefanie Matta, Contract Technical Writer, Houston, Texas

Keep to the Point

As you gather information for a technical training project, you should keep your investigation to the point. As you gather data, visualize the primary audience and their need for the information. Make decisions about whether information stays or goes based on this audience. Refer often to the course objectives and keep information only if it is somehow related to those objectives.

Basic Rule

Above all else, you must keep the objectives of the course in mind as you sift through and organize course materials. As you work on each chapter, keep and include materials only if they somehow help to meet the objective of that chapter.

Challenges of Gathering Information

Almost anyone who has worked on a technical training project will agree that there are times when gathering information is one large headache. This section will discuss the challenges of—and solutions to—effectively gathering information.

Limited Sources

This challenge refers to information so obscure that you will not find a Wikipedia page on it. Sometimes technical information for a particular field is so highly specialized that there are really only two or three people in the world who truly understand the topic. Finding these people and, even more significantly, attaining *access* to them can be a challenge.

If your limited source is a person, you can counter this challenge by being prepared. Isolate the questions that must be answered *by this person only*. Find all the possible answers you can on your own. Don't waste your source's time with questions whose answers you can find elsewhere.

It is also a good idea to ask your SME how *he or she* finds information. Having access to your SME's source of information can be very helpful. Sometimes, for example, your SME may know of an internal server or an external blog that can give you at least a general picture of a particular technical topic.

Missing or Unequal Information

There will be instances in which you have loads of information available (in excruciating detail) about one particular topic, but for a second topic you will have hardly any information at all.

In situations with missing or unequal amounts of information available, understanding and pinpointing what you do and do not have is key. Analyze your outline and, if necessary, visually or anecdotally depict the amount of information available for one topic. (For example, I have 329 pages on Topic A, but I have only 14 pages on Topic B.) Explain this to your SME and then ask for suggestions on where you might find additional information.

Noted

Realize that when you are developing a course, most SMEs will probably overlook key bits of information that they simply view as common knowledge.

—Kenny Amend, Area Manager, Weatherford International, Houston, Texas

Beware of the temptation to simply spend more class time on the topic with the most information available. If a topic warrants it, class time should be spent on it; however, the reason for spending the bulk of the class time on a particular topic should be because the *objectives* call for it, not because that topic has the information easiest to attain.

Inconsistent Information Available

In the process of gathering technical information, sometimes you will find sources that contradict each other. It can be challenging to determine the absolute correct answer. Inconsistent information can occur for various reasons. Sometimes it is a result of the issue being unresolved. Sometimes it is because, after a change has occurred, no one has gotten around to updating all the various sources in which this information resides.

In situations in which you've found inconsistent information, it is best to place the sources next to each other and ask the experts. Let your SMEs battle it out and then give you a final answer.

In addition, you should be open to the fact that information sometimes appears inconsistent because, in certain situations, more than one acceptable solution exists.

Noted

For political or safety-related issues, make sure to get a response clarifying the inconsistency in writing, or follow up with an email about the verbal discussion. If inconsistent information is out there, and you are questioned about why you chose one particular source over another, you will be better off if you can document your reasons.

Mistrust

Some people want to know every possible thing you may do with a particular piece of information before they let you have access to it. It can take time for you to build trust and to explain your intentions. Unfortunately, this can put a damper on your information-gathering efficiencies.

If you are dealing with a person who is distrustful of you or your purpose, your best bet is to take a deep breath and practice patience. Explain as best you can what you are doing. Some people do not like to feel out of control of situations, so recognize this and try to give them an idea of what to expect. If possible, show them one of your other finished projects so they can understand the reasons behind your questions. Sometimes seeing a finished product can help ease some of the distrust.

Technical Jargon

Highly specialized topics are often accompanied by their own "language," complete with dense descriptions and acronyms galore. (I once had to create a class that had an accompanying internal acronym dictionary more than 50 pages long!) Technical jargon can slow down your information gathering, and it can make it difficult to realize what a source is really saying.

Technical jargon can be countered most basically by attaining an industry dictionary or an acronym dictionary. If these items do not exist, start your own. As you come across definitions for these tricky words, phrases, and letters, keep a log of them. Ask other developers with whom you work to do the same, and gradually you will be able to handle the technical jargon better.

Proprietary Material

Technology is pretty much the bread and butter of technical organizations, and organizations usually take precautions to keep proprietary information from getting into unwanted hands. Unfortunately for you, this could include the training department. It can be surprising to see the number of organizations that ask for training on a product without releasing any information about that product, even *internally*. Still, intellectual property management is a serious matter, and therefore some organizations require stringent controls on information.

You can counter the proprietary material challenge by explaining that you will not release the material to any unauthorized people. Offer to put this promise in writing. Explain to the proprietary material holders that they are putting their learners at a disadvantage by withholding important information. You might reference the analogy of attempting to explain swimming to someone without being able to discuss what water is.

Another option is to ask the person worried about releasing the information to become the individual in charge of coming up with a solution. For example, you might ask: "We have established that our target audience needs to know about this technology. I realize that security is an issue; how do *you* suggest that we counter this?" Often this person will find a work-around, and it will be a great idea, because, well, it is his or hers.

And finally, if these tactics don't work, you may just have to accept the fact that some material is simply too sensitive for the general training public of your organization. Figure out what you can and cannot include, and then find a way to work with it.

You Don't Know What to Ask

When our knowledge of a topic is elementary, we don't know what we don't know. This can make it difficult to ask good questions.

This challenge, however, can be met relatively easily. Simply ask your SME this basic question: "What other questions do you think I should be asking you that I am not?"

You Don't Know What You Have

You may have potentially the best source ever, but if your lack of knowledge prevents you from understanding what a treasure of a resource you have, that resource may be overlooked.

In these instances, your best line of defense is to be extra aware that you may be sitting on a gold mine. Asking your SME if he or she notices anything that you have overlooked about a particular source can also be helpful.

Basic Rule
In the event that you lack knowledge about a technical topic, you need to be extra careful that you don't discount potentially useful sources.

Getting It Done

Gathering information for your technical training project is a necessary, but challenging, aspect of technical course development. In general, you should first catalogue the information you have, thinking about it in terms of the "types" of information (for example, categories, levels of information, definitions, components, relationships, analogies, and processes). You need to access as many internal and external sources of information as you can find. When you do find a valid source of information that helps to meet course objectives in some way, you should maximize this material and organize it in a logical manner. There are many challenges to gathering information, but every challenge can be met if you keep a persistent attitude.

Worksheet 5–1. Gathering Information

The following is a worksheet that you can use to determine the current state of data gathering and your future actions related to it.

1. What type of information do I currently possess?

2. What information do I still need?

3. What sources can I tap to find this information?

Worksheet 5–2. Potential Sources of Information

This form can be used when you are at a standstill in gathering information. Go over the following list with your SME.

Do any of the following items exist for our technical topic?

- ✓ facts
- ✓ case examples
- ✓ diagrams
- ✓ definitions
- ✓ processes
- ✓ best practices
- ✓ contingencies
- ✓ components
- ✓ descriptions of internal functioning
- ✓ typical errors
- ✓ calculations
- ✓ paperwork
- ✓ charts
- ✓ graphs
- ✓ equations

- ✓ animations
- ✓ videos
- ✓ scientific principles
- ✓ troubleshooting or decision trees
- ✓ applications
- ✓ limitations
- ✓ features
- ✓ benefits
- ✓ systems
- ✓ job conditions
- ✓ guidelines
- ✓ rules of thumb
- ✓ maintenance procedures
- ✓ service procedures
- ✓ assembly instructions

- ✓ disassembly instructions
- ✓ available upgrades
- ✓ checklists, accessories
- ✓ toolface or equipment readings
- ✓ pre- and post-job checks
- ✓ operational steps or events
- ✓ functions
- ✓ safety issues
- ✓ menus
- ✓ diagrams
- ✓ models
- ✓ illustrations

6

Working with Subject Matter Experts

What's Inside This Chapter

In this chapter, you'll learn

▶ typical course development process flow with an SME
▶ how to prepare your SME for the course development project
▶ specific tactics for collecting information from an SME
▶ how to get past tangents
▶ methods for going through edits with your SME.

One of the most important and distinguishing aspects of technical training is extreme dependence on subject matter experts (SMEs). Because technical courses are designed based on the information given from an SME, we are inherently dependent on the SME (and sometimes all of the SME's idiosyncrasies) when designing a course. In fact, as the topics get more complicated, the "secret" to instructional design becomes more and more about productive work habits and communication with your SME.

When developing a technical training course with an SME, you must be able to adequately prepare the SME for what to expect with the project. You need to have ready a variety of tactics for gathering information, and you need to be able to review content effectively and efficiently with your SME. Each of these items will be discussed in this chapter.

Typical Process Flow

Whether you are working with an SME or not, the typical process flow of a course development project follows the ADDIE model: Analyze, Design, Develop, Implement, and Evaluate.

Although the steps can feel very different from project to project when working with an SME, the ADDIE process is always basically the same and is an excellent method for determining the method of your project's development. A sample of the ADDIE process as applied to course development is seen in Figure 6–1.

Analyze/Design Stage

In this process, the analyze stage and design stage are combined—usually because both of these stages of the process are accomplished in the first couple of meetings between the SME and the developer.

As part of the analyze and design step, the developer sets up a meeting with the SME to determine the overall business purpose and the audience of the class. This is the initial course design meeting that was discussed earlier in this book. In the initial course design meeting, the developer creates the roadmap for the course.

Development Stage

This is the "meat and potatoes" of the course development process. Most of your work and communication with the SME will occur in this stage of the process. At this point, the initial course design meeting has taken place, and the direction of the project has been set.

Within this stage, the SME begins to release technical information for the course to the developer. This data is preliminary information only and is usually some technical data related to the course that will get the developer started. As the developer gets to work on the preliminary data, the SME, in the meantime, usually has a "homework" list of information to gather for the developer. That is, the SME must essentially gather the missing pieces of technical information needed to complete a draft of the course.

Figure 6–1. Typical Course Development Process Flow with an SME

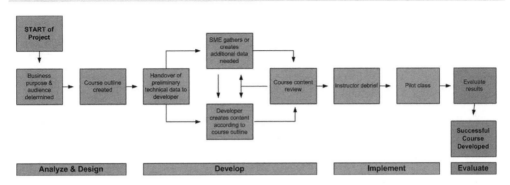

Once the SME has supplied all of the necessary information, the developer puts together a first draft. This draft is then reviewed by the SME. The SME makes comments on incorrect, incomplete, unnecessary, or insufficient information. The developer takes these comments and updates the training material for a second draft, which is then resubmitted to the SME for approval. This leads to a third draft, and so on. In few instances is only one review enough. Usually it takes quite a bit of back-and-forth between the developer and the SME to get a complete, correct finished product.

Noted

Don't get discouraged if it takes multiple edits to get your technical course developed. Multiple edits help to ensure that you have complete, accurate content that is satisfactory for both your needs and those of your SME.

Implementation Stage

In the next step of the ADDIE model, the implementation step, the pilot class is arranged. After the material is finalized, the developer and the instructor (who may also be the SME) usually get together for an *instructor briefing session* to discuss the course content as a whole. This is the time for the developer to ensure that the instructor understands the overall flow of the course, the purpose of the exercises, and so on. Also, this is a great opportunity for you to answer any questions about teaching tools or exercises that you included in the course.

The crux of the implementation stage is the pilot course. This is your opportunity to see the efforts of the development stage come to life. It is important for you to attend this pilot course. You must be able to observe the exercises and the lessons and see how the audience reacts to them. The pilot course is the opportunity for you to see how the class flows, what works, and what doesn't work. In addition, if there are experimental exercises or activities in the course, you may need to stand up and help the instructor explain the instructions for the exercises.

Evaluation Stage

After the pilot course, the evaluation portion of the model takes effect. You are primarily concerned here with determining whether the course objectives were addressed and satisfied, but you will also be looking at the flow of the class, audience reaction, effectiveness of exercises, and effectiveness of the instructor. In addition, postcourse evaluations are completed by the participants, and other relevant measurements are conducted, such as pre- and postcourse comprehension tests. The developer and the SME look at all these items to evaluate the effectiveness of the course in its present form and to see if any material within the course needs to be adjusted. If everything checks out, the project at this point is successfully completed.

Understanding how the ADDIE process is applied to projects in which an SME is part of the formula is important. Although every technical training project is unique, projects should essentially follow the steps described above. Each step may feel a little different or may be carried out slightly differently depending on the SME and the technical topic, but the overall process should remain intact. Understanding the ADDIE model when you are presented with an SME as part of the project team helps you to be prepared for what to expect during the project.

Noted

As you go through the ADDIE process, you may find it helpful to document details of the process into some sort of record-keeping document. This can help you stay on track if you are juggling multiple projects. A clear description of each meeting and major work milestone can help clear up any areas where there may be confusion or discrepancies about what was agreed. Also, if for some reason the project must be put on hold, you will be able to get yourself quickly back on track when the project is reinstated. You can use whatever record-keeping tactic you find most convenient. You can also integrate this record-keeping within the organizational structure you have developed to organize your materials. The important thing is that you choose a system that works for you and stick with it.

Preparing SMEs for the Project

It is important to effectively prepare your SME for the course development project. There are a few things you should do to facilitate an effective working relationship with your SME.

At the onset of the project, take some time to get to know your SME and build rapport. Talk about his or her background and what led him or her to this particular position. Try to determine the personal stake that your SME has in the project. Discuss his or her communication preferences—that is, does he or she prefer that you contact him or her by phone or email, and is morning or afternoon better, for example? You can even find out a little bit about your SME's interests and hobbies. Most important, however, at the onset of development, you should at some point explain to your SME the roles of those involved in the project, what is expected of the SME, what to expect during the project, and the type of information you will be seeking as the project progresses. These items will be discussed below.

Explaining Roles

When beginning a technical course development project, it is important that the SME understand the role of the SME and the role of the designer. Chapter 2 went into details on the two roles; but essentially, it is important that the SME understand that there are two sides—the technical side and the educational side—that come together to create a complete product. Your role as the developer is to provide the framework, structure, and sound educational foundation for the learning material; the SME's job as the technical expert is to provide the content. The SME has the final say in *what* is said, but you have the final say in *how* it is said.

Just as you will have to learn something about the technical content, your SME should learn about your role. You should explain the many recent advances in the educational field and the fact that as training is very expensive to develop, it makes sense to use these advances to the best of our abilities. You can explain that people's learning preferences differ, that adults usually respond better to a facilitation type of instruction, and that to reach a multicultural, multigenerational audience, you must employ certain development tactics.

Noted

An SME's Perspective

Understanding the SME's preconceived ideas will also help prepare the SME for the instructional process. Some difficult barriers can be eliminated if the notion of "training as usual," that is, "training as just a passive PowerPoint lecture," is addressed. Don't be fooled! The SME has a plan, which, if it is not exactly what yours is, could spell trouble.

—Kenny Amend, Area Manager, Weatherford International, Houston, Texas

Explaining What Is Expected of the SME

It is only fair that the SME understand what will be expected of him or her as the project progresses. Explain that the following points are important:

The SME should keep an open mind. The instructional design process may seem foreign to your SME, but keeping an open mind helps move the process along. This is important, especially when the SME will be the instructor for the course. The SME may be highly protective of his or her way of teaching and may need help to become more flexible.

The SME should return information on time. You are both working on a timetable, and for the process to continue smoothly, it is extremely important that information be supplied by the agreed-on deadlines. If there is a delay for some reason, this should be communicated as soon as possible.

The SME should make decisions. Because the SME is the one in charge of the substance of the course, it is extremely important that he or she make decisions on issues of content and stick to them. Communicate the importance of this.

The SME should provide lots of materials in the beginning. At the beginning of a project, if the SME can go through his or her files and hand over any relevant documents, presentations, graphics, or videos, these items will help immensely.

The SME should keep up his or her professional knowledge. The technical knowledge and the professional relationships of the SME form your pathway to the content. If there is a legit gray area surrounding the content and the SME is not authorized to clear up all issues, the SME should know who to go to in order to get an answer. Your information is only as good as that of your SME, so it is quite important that the SME keep connected and up-to-date on the technical subject.

The SME should remember that everyone involved in the project has a specific role. Ask the SME to try to understand your perspective. As much as necessary, remind the SME of both of your roles and how both roles affect the project.

Explaining the Process

It is also helpful to describe to the SME what to expect during the process. You can describe the ADDIE model and explain that you will be going through all of these steps together. Give specifics about what will be covered during each step of this process. From the SME's perspective, understanding that there is a method to the course development madness can help him or her to buy into your vision for the course.

Explaining the Type of Information You Need

You should also prep the SME on what kind of information you are likely to be seeking as the course design process progresses. As you begin to ask question after question about the content of the course, it will help if your SME understands why you are asking these questions. Explain that you will be looking at the material from a different angle than the SME does, and as such, your questions sometimes might seem a little odd. Explain that you will be seeking answers about

- ▶ categories
- ▶ levels of information
- ▶ definitions
- ▶ components
- ▶ relationships
- ▶ analogies
- ▶ processes.

It will make the course development process easier if your SME understands that sometimes the questions you pose are asked because you are trying to determine whether particular pieces of information are parallel concepts, organized into the correct category, completely described, covered under the objectives of the course, or organized in a logical order (as discussed previously in chapter 5, "Gathering Information"). If you can, try to get your SME to see what you mean by showing him or her an organized—and then an unorganized—topic list you have completed for a previous project so your SME can see the end that you have in mind. You can refer to Figure 4–6 for an example.

Noted

Sometimes SMEs can become suspicious of the inquisitiveness of a technical course developer. Especially if an SME is also the instructor, an SME can feel threatened or that his or her expertise is being challenged as the technical developer proceeds with his or her interrogation. This can lead to a "cooling" of communication between the SME and the developer and can severely affect the process. The SME must understand that only through this exchange of information and ideas can the technical design process succeed.

Think About This

It's important that you gain buy-in from your SME early in the process. "Buy-in" occurs at the exact moment the SME decides that your vision for the course is actually not a challenge to his or her expertise or a tedious annoyance, but rather a well-thought-out effort to make the material and course more easily understandable for the target audience and more effective overall. When an SME reaches this conclusion, he or she has officially "bought in" to the development process.

It is important that you do whatever you must to gain buy-in from your SME. You can accomplish this in various ways:

- Ask someone with whom you have already worked to talk to your new SME. This person can vouch for your good work and may possibly be able to explain how the development process works and how helpful it was.

- If you have management support, you can have your SME's manager put in a good word about how the instructional design process produces a quality product.

- You can show your SME examples of your past work. If you have an example of a course that you have already done, showing it to your SME may help him or her understand just what you are trying to accomplish. Demonstrating to your SME that you are capable of producing a quality project can help him or her to trust you. In addition, it can get your SME excited about the prospect of a polished finished course of his or her own.

- Look at your SME as an individual. Think about what is likely to motivate your SME, and then relate the finished product of your course to those motivational factors. You will probably need to find something different for each SME.

Specific Tactics for Collecting Information

There are specific tactics that you can use to obtain data from your SME. These tactics include asking pointed questions, creating a to-do list, developing exploratory worksheets, utilizing existing job materials, creating a skeleton PowerPoint, hosting a content design meeting, and holding a pilot course. These tactics are explained in detail below.

Pointed Questions

As a non-SME, you can go about attaining information for a technical course in many ways. The most obvious tactic is to simply ask questions. Of course, there is a caveat to this seemingly basic strategy: You must do your research first. Figure out what you can on your own. Don't ask a question whose answer you can find for yourself. SMEs are busy people, and you can lose a lot of credibility by asking questions whose answers are easily found in books, online, or through other "easy" resources. So do yourself a favor and build up credit for those questions to which you really need an answer.

Basic Rule

Don't waste time asking SMEs questions whose answers you can find yourself!

Noted

A question posed to an SME concerning where information can be found is *always* a legitimate question.

To-Do List

Another simple tactic you can use to gain information from your SME is to create a "to-do list" for missing information you need from your SME. This allows the SME to see everything he or she is responsible for in order to complete the project. In addition, these lists can be helpful because they are a documented record of the project's status. The downside of the to-do list is that, like a lot of other things, the list can simply fall by the wayside. The SME may look at the list and forget what the to-dos mean. For example, when talking to you, the concept of "an exercise explaining the purpose of the hydraulics program" may have made sense to him or her; however, when the SME is on his or her own going back to the list, these items can be hard to remember, and thus the SME will just ignore them.

To prevent the SME from forgetting what the items on the to-do list refer to, you can help by being more specific and descriptive in what you put on the list and how you present it. If you have a sample completed exercise for a different topic that gets at the same concept, submit that, along with your to-do list, as an example to show that "this is the type of thing I am seeking."

Noted

Just as there is a to-do list for the SME, you should have your own to-do list that contains the items for which you are responsible. Complete everything that you can with the information currently available to you. Ideally, you will always have all the to-dos done that you can do on your own.

Basic Rule

Keep up-to-date on your end. You should always have your to-dos completed and waiting for the SME.

SME Worksheets

In conjunction with the to-do list is the tactic of creating documentation, or "paper ways," to get information. Consider creating general worksheets that your SME can fill out. For example, let's say you need operational information on things that can go wrong on a job and how to fix them. You might give your SME a worksheet like the one in Figure 6–2. From the answers the SME supplies by filling out this chart (or another one), you have the missing information you need for the course.

Figure 6–2. Sample SME Worksheet

Think about what our target audience needs to know in order to troubleshoot effectively. What are the *most* important issues that can come up during a job? Please fill out the chart below.

	What Can Go Wrong?	How to Fix It
1.		
2.		
3.		

Existing Job Materials

In addition, you can refer to existing job examples for information. *Job material* refers to the paper trail left when a service is ordered or performed. Typically, this paperwork is readily available from the organization and contains a wealth of information about the task, such as items that were needed before the service was performed, how long the service took, what materials were needed during the service, and what tasks the service provider performed.

This job material can be invaluable, and it can save time for your SME by giving him or her a starting point for various course exercises or examples. Your SME can use this existing job example or can edit the job example to make an alternate case study. Regardless of how your SME decides to use the job information, have him or her walk you through the thought process of putting the job together, step by step. Write down relevant teaching points or technical questions to ask (with answers) during each part of the process.

Skeleton PowerPoints

Using your outline, you can also create a skeleton PowerPoint for your SME to fill out (Figure 6–3). Many SMEs are comfortable using PowerPoint as a tool, so you might as well use it. This does not mean, however, that the PowerPoint your SME

Figure 6–3. Sample Skeleton PowerPoint Slides

	Product #1: Basic Information	Product #1: Internal Components
• Instructor: Please fill out the information asked for in this presentation.	• Define the purpose of this product. • What are the features, benefits and applications? • Copy and paste an image of this product.	• List the internal components. • Define the purpose and benefit of each component. • Describe how the components interact. • Copy and paste an image of each component (insert new slides as necessary).
Product #1: Operation • What preparation needs to take place before operating this product? • Describe each step of operation. • What can go wrong on the job? Why? How might you fix this?	**Product #1: Sample Scenario** • Describe a scenario where this product was successfully used on a job.	**Product #1: Savings and Value** • Describe the various ways that this product can provide savings and value to the customer.
Product #2: Basic Information • Define the purpose of this product. • What are the features, benefits and applications? • Copy and paste an image of this product.	**Product #2: Internal Components** • List the internal components. • Define the purpose and benefit of each component. • Describe how the components interact. • Copy and paste an image of each component (insert new slides as necessary).	**Product #2: Operation** • What preparation needs to take place before operating this product? • Describe each step of operation. • What can go wrong on the job? Why? How might you fix this?
Product #2: Sample Scenario • Describe a scenario where this product was successfully used on a job.	**Product #2: Savings and Value** • Describe the various ways that this product can provide savings and value to the customer.	**Additional Information** • Is there any other relevant information that we need to include about product #1 or product #2? What and why?

creates will end up being the final project. Once you get the information you need, you can rework the presentation, you can move the relevant material to the manual, or you can use the content to create interactive exercises and worksheets.

Content Development Meetings

SMEs are busy people, and like most busy people, as they sit down at their desks, they are likely to be bombarded with a million other things to do. While your project may be important, they may find it difficult to simply drop everything and pound out responses to your to-do list.

One way you can increase the amount of information you receive is by holding *content development meetings*. Content development meetings are preset work sessions in which you and your SME(s) come together and actually produce the information you need right then and there in the meeting room. These specific meetings can be helpful, because they force the SME to set aside time to finish the things you need for the course. During these meetings, it may be useful to set out worksheets for the SME(s) to fill out.

Pilot Course

And then, if all else fails, you can throw the pilot course at your SME. There is nothing like a deadline to make your project a priority. Scheduling a pilot course can get you the information you need very quickly—especially if your SME will be the person responsible for teaching the class. You can manage this "rush" pilot course by restricting who is allowed in and limiting advertising for the course. Think of it as a "soft opening." During this pilot course, you will quickly learn what is working and what is not, as well as what you need to expand and what you need to limit. The vast majority of the time, participants who attend pilot courses are very perceptive and open about suggesting and supplying additional exercises and information to include.

In summary, you may find that to be successful, you must use one or a combination of the tactics described above. Do what works for your particular SME and for your particular situation. Be adaptable. There is no one best way that will help you attain the information you need. It is through constant and effective communication with your SME that you are likely to find the right fit for both of you.

Getting Past Tangents

Sometimes, when communicating with your SME, you are bound to find yourself faced with an issue that can easily become the bane of a technical developer's existence: the Dreaded SME Tangent.

Most everyone who has designed a technical course has been frustrated by the long-winded tangents on various technical topics that some SMEs have the tendency to proclaim. Little will bring a productive meeting to a grinding halt faster than an SME pontificating on some bizarre kernel of information that is of limited relevance to your course, but on the subject of which the SME is highly educated and excited to share. Tangents can bog down a meeting, frustrate you, confuse you, and possibly even bore you to tears.

Still, there is a positive side to tangents.

Sometimes tangents can clue you in on missing course objectives. Consider this quote from an SME's perspective:

Typically when an SME goes on a tangent/tirade it is because there may be information missing that was not identified in the outline. The SME may have just realized that more information will be required than was determined at the onset of the course development project. (Kenny Amend, Area Manager, Weatherford International)

In addition, as much as you may want to gather information in a linear fashion, there are instances when it is valuable to just let the information flow in naturally. Be on the lookout for spontaneous tidbits that you can catch as you go. SMEs are not necessarily thinking in the context of a class as they are explaining things to you. As the SME speaks, be mindful of information that might be related to a different part of the course and document it. Don't be afraid to switch gears temporarily if you suddenly realize you are listening to golden information for a different section of the course. You may never get back to this same conversation, and thus you may not have easy access again to the explanation being given. As long as you realize that you and your SME are on a tangent, and you make a mental (or physical) note of where the conversation branched off, you are still in good shape and can set yourself up to capture many valuable nuggets of information.

This is not to say, however, that you should be a slave to the aimlessly wandering minds of all SMEs or that you should always let them decide where the conversation goes. If a tangent gets out of control or an SME keeps returning to it unnecessarily, first look critically at the topic and make sure there is not a connection you are missing. If there is no connection the SME can adequately explain and you are certain it is a "rogue tangent," cut it off as best you can. Comments such as these may work: "I understand that may be part of the third chapter. We will get to that shortly. For now, I need information for chapter 2," or "According to the objectives we came up with for this class, that information is not included. Either we have to rethink our objectives or that material likely has a spot in an entirely different class. I will make a note of it, and we can return to it later. For now, I am interested in these things listed for chapter 2." These comments can help you recover from the tangent of a wayward SME.

Despite the risk of rogue tangents, digressions from the topic can, if managed and used correctly, provide unprecedented access to information. Recognizing the value of a tangent is a skill set that every technical developer needs to hone. If you should choose not to engage in a tantalizing tangent because of time or other constraints, at the very least, write down as many key phrases as you can that might help you to spur this conversation with the SME later. Even though you may not fully understand the thought process that spurred the SME to go off on a specific tangent (as far as all the intricacies and relatedness of the technical topic), it is important to be able to recognize the signs of a valuable information drop and tap into these opportunities.

Not all tangents will lead you to a pot of gold. Still, recognizing when to let a tangent run wild can provide you with a valuable occasion for collecting missing information.

Going Through Edits with Your SME

After you have successfully collected information from your SME and put together a first draft of the training materials, you will eventually need to schedule a review session with your SME. While there is likely to be relief on your side that you were able to get a first draft finished, your development work is unfortunately not finished. It is necessary that the SME review the content, edit it, and clearly communicate any changes necessary for the material.

Noted

Sometimes the SME will review the material on his or her own, and sometimes you and the SME will go through it together. What is important is that you possess a complete understanding of the edits the SME has made; whether this is accomplished via email or face-to-face depends on you and the situation.

Your editing sessions with your SME can be quite extensive. You are basically asking him or her to consider whether course objectives will be met through the training content provided, whether there is a logical flow of material, whether technical explanations are complete and unnecessary information is removed, and, finally, whether the course exercises are challenging and useful. You should look positively on review sessions with your SME; you will have the opportunity to heighten the value of your class.

As you review material with an SME, you should ask pointed questions in order to facilitate a higher quality of content:

- ▶ What are your overall impressions of the material?
- ▶ Does this material meet our objectives?

- What are the weak points of the section? What are the strong points?
- Does this exercise make sense here?
- How is the flow of the section? Should any concepts be rearranged? Does it make sense to talk about Idea X before we begin talking about Idea Y?
- Are we missing anything in this section?
- What do you think is the most important part of this section? Are we covering it well enough?
- What do you think the learners will have the hardest time understanding? Is there anything we can do to help them understand it better?
- We need some interactivity in the class. Do you have any ideas? What would make a good exercise?
- If you could talk about only one thing in this chapter, what would it be?
- If you had to take one thing out of the chapter (because of time constraints or some other circumstance), what would it be? Why?
- What do you think is the most controversial part of the material? Are we addressing it in the right way? In what other ways might we address it?
- If learners could take only one thing out of this section, what would it be?
- Is there any material that is not absolute, that is, is there any content that does not specifically have a yes or no or right or wrong answer? Are we addressing it in the right way? Should we ask an open-ended question about it? Should we have a planned exercise in class in which learners debate both sides of the issue?
- Does this sentence make sense? How might I word it better?
- Could you take this marker and highlight the main points of the section for a summary I am writing?

Noted

If a concept is difficult for an SME to explain, this may signal to you that more exercises, pictures, animations, and so on are needed than previously thought.

Dealing with Items Removed from the Material

Your SME ultimately has the responsibility for whether or not something stays in the material. Don't become so attached to the content you created that you are not able to take constructive criticism or say "good-bye" to something you created for the course. You should be able to look at the content as an outsider.

In saying this, it is still acceptable to question why something stays or why something is removed—especially if it is something you feel is necessary to the course. As you are an outsider to the technical content, sometimes you have a good perspective that will match that of the eventual learners.

Ensuring that Grammar and Paragraph Structure Make Sense

Another aspect to be aware of when going through edits with your SME is verifying that the entire paragraph or section still makes sense when the SME crosses out material. Sometimes, an SME will cross out something that is not true. This is good. However, sometimes taking out one sentence will change the meaning of the paragraph. You need to look at the point of the deleted sentence and double-check that the paragraph still makes sense. To verify this, simply ask your SME: "If we take that sentence out, does the paragraph still make sense? Does it still flow with the paragraph above? Is there something we could add to make the sentence true?" Sometimes, your SME will then respond with something like "OK, I see what you mean. OK, instead of taking the entire thing out, let's just change 'actual depth' to 'calculated depth' and then we can keep that sentence."

Basically, regardless of whether a particular sentence or paragraph stays or goes, what is important is that the content be accurate per the SME's vetting.

Basic Rule
Your SME has the final say on technical content in the course.

Keeping Old Drafts

As you begin to compile different versions of material from your SME review sessions, it is important to keep old drafts of the material. Prior drafts can clarify the evolution of the course and the material, should questions arise. In addition, you never know when the SME will change his or her mind about an exercise or a chart that was removed, and you can save yourself time and hassle if you are able to quickly copy and paste something your SME wants included after all.

Treat the Topic as an Individual

Finally, remember that every technical subject needs to be treated individually. There are huge differences and variations in technical subject matter, and the type of information provided for one topic may not be available for a second one. Accepting this helps you to make the most out of the content you *do* have available.

Remember Your Strengths

Don't forget that one of your strengths is that you are not an expert on the information you are developing. Because of this, you don't allow your SME to take anything for granted. Your questions force the SME to explain things in a more complete way. Even though SMEs may sound exasperated at times, and you may feel foolish when you realize that you are asking a very basic question that everyone already assumes you know the answer to, remember that to be successful as a designer or a writer, you sometimes just have to ask the question. Someday, with experience, you might get to a high level of understanding on your technical topic. Don't be devastated or disheartened if it doesn't happen overnight. It took these people years to become SMEs. No one expects you to do it overnight.

If it helps you to feel better about yourself, decorate your workspace with reminders of all the things you do well in order to remind yourself—after a long afternoon of feeling like a clueless idiot about a technical process—that you are good at other things. All expertise is relative. The fact that you do not know about a certain technical process does not make you stupid. It just means you don't know about that particular technical process—nothing more, and nothing less. Besides, you'll probably find, just from the nature of learning, that you will know a whole lot more about that technical process than the average person by the time you have finished developing the course.

Basic Rule

You can be successful as a developer without being an expert on the technical material.

Getting It Done

It cannot be emphasized enough that being able to work effectively with an SME is a critical skill for a nontechnical designer who is designing a highly technical training course. In highly technical, highly specialized trades, you will not necessarily find a library of knowledge where you can go to find information or look up the answers to your questions. You are dependent on another person, an expert, to provide this information to you. Therefore your relationship with this person and your communication with this person are very important. As such, when you are designing technical training classes, communication skills become just as important as knowing instructional design theory.

There are various tactics you can use in order to draw information from an SME. The most obvious include asking questions and determining whether to let technical tangents run their course. You can also create to-do lists, distribute SME worksheets, review past jobs as a potential starting point, create skeleton PowerPoints, host a content development meeting, or hold a pilot course.

When reviewing material with your SME, you are basically asking him or her to consider whether course objectives will be met through the training content provided, whether there is a logical flow of material, whether technical explanations are complete and unnecessary information is removed, and, finally, whether the course exercises are challenging and useful. You should look positively on review sessions with your SME, as these provide an opportunity to heighten the value of your class.

In addition, as a nontechnical developer, you bring a fresh perspective to the material. Your questions force the SME to consider important holes in the material that might otherwise have been overlooked.

Finally, you will find that what works for one project and one SME does not always work for your next project and your next SME. It is through constant and effective communication with your SME that you are likely to find the right fit for both of you each time.

Worksheet 6–1. The Course Development SME Handout

The following is a handout that you can copy for your SME to use as talking points at the beginning of a project.

Thanks for partnering on this project. Here is a little information about what to expect.

Roles:

You bring the technical side to the development, and I bring the instructional side. We each bring valuable perspectives and together will produce a superior product because of this.

About the process:

We will be using the ADDIE model. This involves the following steps:

1. Analyzing
2. Designing
3. Developing
4. Implementing
5. Evaluating

I look at the material from a different angle. I may ask odd questions because I am looking for

* categories
* levels of information
* definitions
* components
* relationships
* analogies
* processes.

What you can do:

- Keep an open mind. This process may seem strange at first, but every step has a specific point. We are going to create a class that meets both business needs and learner needs.

- Meet deadlines. We are working on a timetable, and for the process to continue smoothly, it is important that information be supplied by the agreed-on deadlines. If there is a holdup for some reason, this should be communicated as soon as possible.

- Make decisions. Because you are the one in charge of technical content, it is extremely important that you make decisions and stick to them.

- Provide lots of resources. As we begin the project, if you find any relevant documents, presentations, graphics, or videos, these can help immensely for my work flow.

- Stay current. Your technical knowledge and professional relationships are my pathway to content. Your knowledge of whom to go to in the event that you don't know an answer is just as valuable as knowing the answer itself. For a successful outcome of the course, it is important that you keep connected and up-to-date on the technical subject.

- Remember our roles. When we combine your technical knowledge with my instructional knowledge, a truly great and useful product can be created.

Thanks, and I look forward to working with you!

Worksheet 6–2. SME Editing Criteria

The following is a handout that you can copy for your SME as editing criteria for a project review.

Thank you again for your help in providing technical expertise for this project. As you review the training documentation, please use the checklist below.

- Objectives are met.
- There is no logical flow of material.
- Explanations are complete.
- Unnecessary information is removed.
- Exercises are challenging and tied to objectives.

Regarding the topics above, please note that it is up to you to provide detailed explanations referencing specific areas of the material so that I can successfully make the necessary edits.

The items below in gray are examples of poor edits. I do not know what should go in place of the item you crossed out, and the indication of "not correct" is not specific enough for me to know what to change.

There should be five components attached to the front section of the ~~mandrel~~. You can determine which component is the prime power source by attaching a hydraulic hose filled with fluid 74-b. not correct

---

The following items in gray are examples of good edits! The comments were very specific and clear. I know exactly what should be changed and communication is on track.

There should be five components attached to the front section of the ~~mandrel~~ hydraulic tank. You can determine which component is the prime power source by attaching a hydraulic hose filled with fluid ~~74-b~~ 74-a.

Thank you again for your time, and please do not hesitate to contact me with any questions.

Worksheet 6–3. Determine Your Tactics

Please fill out the following form in order to determine which tactics from the chapter you will apply to your situation.

How will I explain my role to my SME?

In what way(s) will I gain buy-in from my SME?

What are two tactics I will apply when gathering information or reviewing information with my SME?

7

Designing Classroom Exercises for Highly Technical Content

What's Inside This Chapter

In this chapter, you'll learn

- ▶ why activity is important
- ▶ three categories of exercises
- ▶ how to build a library of examples
- ▶ exercise ideas
- ▶ how to take a critical look at exercises.

Good training helps companies develop happy and productive workers. If organizations are going to spend thousands of dollars on conducting training for their employees and thousands more in lost productivity from taking employees away from their jobs for training, then they need to maximize their return on that considerable investment. Organizations need to make sure they are doing everything they can to ensure that the training is useful, that they are using the most modern teaching methods, and that their employees are getting the most out of their class and time away from work. Incorporating useful exercises into the course can accomplish this.

This chapter will discuss aspects related to designing valuable classroom exercises for highly technical content.

Why Activity Is Important

We all remember "the 100 percent lecture course"—that mind-numbing classroom experience in which a professor droned on for hours and the only break in the monotony was the clicking of a PowerPoint slide or the ticking of the slowly moving wall-hung clock. Sadly, many technical training courses mirror this experience.

There is a myth that telling equals training (Hannum, 2009). However, there is a difference between a learner *listening* to information and a learner actually *acquiring* knowledge (Hannum, 2009). The act of sitting in a classroom and listening or observing a class is called passive learning. Active learning is the opposite. Active learning involves participation in activities and the compelling of learners to engage in the subject matter itself. Examples of active learning include completing a worksheet, participating in class discussion, working through a simulation, and so on. The consensus of the training industry is that effective training courses incorporate active learning principles.

Basic Rule
Active learning activities and exercises should be included in your course.

Lecture can be useful and does have its place in training, but as lecture tends to be grossly overrepresented, its usage must be minimized. You can include a passive learning element such as lecture or direct instruction in your course, but it needs to be managed properly. The next section explains why.

The Primacy-Recency Effect

In 1962, a psychologist named Bennet Murdock conducted an experiment in which he gave participants a list of items to memorize. When Murdock later asked these participants to recall the items on the list, he discovered an interesting phenomenon. Across the board, participants tended to remember the same items from the list. Specifically, they tended to remember items at the beginning and the end of the list, with their recall of items in the middle tapering off. This effect, known as the serial position effect, or primacy-recency effect, is of particular interest to those who develop technical training.

Incorporating the Primacy-Recency Effect

To best benefit from the primacy-recency effect in your course design, you must abstain from including long, drawn-out lectures in the class. As noted, the primacy-recency effect explains that the learner's retention is greatest for information at the beginning and end of a section. Thus, there is a lack of retention for material in the gulf between those two points. The longer the lecture, the greater the gulf between beginning and end. If you want to give learners the best chance to remember something in a class, you need to limit lecture to short segments and provide activities (breaks) in between. These breaks in the lecture function as starting and stopping points, or beginnings and endings, thus giving the learners more of a chance to remember items covered within the lecture portions of the class.

Consider this example. With a three-hour lecture that includes no activities, learners are given only one beginning (primacy effect) and one end (recency effect) through which to remember information. Thus, we are giving learners only two chances to maximize their retention (see Figure 7–1). If, however, that three-hour lecture is roughly broken into half-hour segments interspersed with activities, as in Figure 7–2, the learners are given six beginnings and six ends, or a total of 12 opportunities to maximize retention. From this example, it is clear that by segmenting lecture with activities, you are giving learners more beginning and end points at which to remember information.

Figure 7–1. Straight Lecture

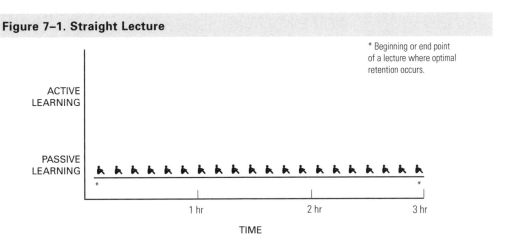

* Beginning or end point of a lecture where optimal retention occurs.

ACTIVE LEARNING

PASSIVE LEARNING

1 hr   2 hr   3 hr

TIME

Figure 7–2. Lecture Broken Apart With Activities

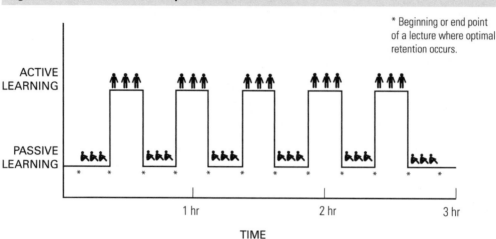

Activities

It is not difficult to look at the research (and your own experiences) and determine that lecture—by itself—does not make for an effective course. Activity is crucial for any classroom, especially one with subject matter as difficult and complex as that found in technical training courses. Remember, with "activity" we are not talking about "Let's all get up and stretch" or "15 minutes for coffee and bathroom breaks." We're talking about active learning sessions—exercises, group problem solving, or critical thinking sessions that use different learning techniques and engage the learners' brains in ways beyond passive listening.

But what kinds of activities are necessary in a training course? The simple answer is any and all that help to meet the course objectives. Research shows that it is not so much the specific type of interactivity that is significant, but more that interactivity in general is incorporated into the learning. This interactivity can include worksheets, review questions, group work, presentations, brainstorming, hands-on practicals, or case studies.

Basically, if you have incorporated a variety of learning methods within your class, you have created an effective environment (Lalley & Miller, 2007).

Noted

An SME's Perspective on Interactive Training

My first challenge in training was to develop a course about the equipment and services I had spent learning for the previous 20+ years. The course ended up being packed with information, and all who attended were subjected to 4.5 days of cruel lecture. It wasn't long before I realized one critical point in my lecture-laden course was being overlooked: Not much was being learned by the participants. There may have been a few important facts or methods that a few learners took away from the course, but the learned things were varied and inconsistent. What was the problem? Bad instructor? Bad information? Poor writing? Maybe a little of all of those?

I realized that the system we were following created a course where it was more about how much the instructor knew and how he presented it than it was about the learner and what the learner took away and retained. This needed to change.

My first experience working with instructional developers was as a director of training for a global company. At this point in my career I had seven to eight instructor/SMEs in my group, each having different teaching styles, personalities, and experience levels. Most of the SMEs had been trained to be excellent speakers and lecturers. They all liked to talk, and a few even relished the idea of being the center of attention. Some were great storytellers. Others were marvels when it came to quoting "technical scripture."

The instructional developers began work on a variety of courses with the SMEs in my group. The surprising element the developers brought was the introduction of new (to the group) ways of teaching. Card games, group coursework, exercises, and learner presentations all were suggested and used in pilot courses. Many of the SMEs were skeptical that the typical audience would participate or enjoy the active learning methods being introduced.

By the end of the second course, it was clear that the new methods were very successful and accepted by some of the most avid critics on my staff. Additionally, learners were taking away valuable information and spreading the word that their time was well spent during our technical courses.

I couldn't argue with the results, and everyone on staff agreed that the new course design was more effective than the traditional approach.

—Kenny Amend, Area Manager, Weatherford International, Houston, Texas

Three Categories of Exercises

Exercises may fall into one of three categories. The categories, in ascending order, indicate the amount of technical knowledge necessary to design the activities. Category A exercises are generally related to the subject matter, meaning a developer can typically create these activities with limited involvement of the subject matter expert (SME). Category C exercises are so specifically related to the subject matter that a developer cannot create them without direct input from the SME. Category B exercises are somewhere in between.

Category A

Category A exercises are the easiest and quickest to develop. They are *response-oriented exercises*, meaning that the technical developer poses some sort of question or a subject for discussion, and the learners' exercise is to come up with a response.

These exercises can be easily applied to many situations. The questions posed by the training developer are general enough that they could pertain more or less to any technical product or task.

To generate Category A exercises, think about questions regarding the product or task in a general sense and then write these general questions down in a worksheet. As a developer, you really need no specific technical knowledge to create these types of questions and exercises. The following are examples of Category A exercise questions that incorporate generic language that can apply to multiple topics:

- ▶ List items you need to consider before performing a task.
- ▶ Analyze your job. Describe what can go wrong, why this might happen, and how you could fix it.
- ▶ What information do you need to gather before you perform a task?
- ▶ Name three things that you learned in this section. Describe how they are related to your job.
- ▶ Describe one concept covered in the lecture that you think novice learners might have trouble with. Prepare a five-minute presentation.
- ▶ Choose one concept from the lecture and visually depict it on a poster.

These open-ended Category A exercises tend to work well for experienced and highly motivated learners. With Category A exercises, learners are able to build on their own experience, and they are actually the ones who guide where the learning goes. Category A exercises let the learners' knowledge determine the level of content discussed.

This leads, however, to a possible drawback of Category A exercises. By allowing an individual class to determine what topics are covered, you run the risk of a "runaway classroom" in which the learners take the class so far off track that the training goals suffer. In addition, it can be hard to set consistent standards of what a particular exercise in a course is supposed to cover when responses are allowed to run wild.

Another downside is that the class can be limited by lack of experience. Category A exercises are generally not as effective for inexperienced, novice learners. If learners have little experience to draw on, the discussion will be limited, as will the places that the course can go. The exercises may not lead the learners to the correct objectives.

Still, for motivated and experienced learners, Category A exercises are quite valuable. They allow for the high knowledge level of the learners to enrich the exercise. In addition, Category A exercises are the easiest and least time consuming exercises to develop.

Category B

Category B exercises are specific to a particular technical topic and are more detailed and structured than Category A exercises. Category B exercises may still take the form of a worksheet, but the questions on the worksheet will be more targeted and specific to the topic and the information surrounding the topic.

Figure 7–3 shows an example of the difference between Category A and Category B exercise questions. Category B exercises will require input from your SME. This makes them generally more time-consuming to develop than Category A exercises. In addition, because these exercises are more focused and specific to the technical content, they do not leave as much room for learners to guide their own learning or to further delve into topics of their individual interests.

Figure 7–3. Difference Between Category A and Category B Exercise Questions

Category A	Category B
Question: What can go wrong on a job?	Question: While operating, the pipe separates into two pieces, parting the string. The Outside Diameter of the end piece of pipe that came out of the hole should have been 4-½ in. but instead was measured at 4-⅜ in. What happened, and what should you do next? Why?

Still, Category B exercises can be useful because they can direct learners specifically to various learning points. This can be extremely important when the subject matter is new and the training level of your audience is not as advanced. Category B exercises are good for courses in which your training goals are more focused and targeted. In Category B exercises, the instructor, not the learners, guides the training course toward its objectives.

Category C

Category C exercises involve taking the course content and applying it as closely as possible to a job situation for the target audience. These exercises cannot be completed without the direct input and influence of the SME. If done correctly with the right amount of detail, these exercises—referred to as "case study exercises"—are especially suited for transfer of knowledge to the job.

Noted

Case study exercises are great for discussion and sharing the wealth of knowledge that exists in a room.

—Kenny Amend, Area Manager, Weatherford International, Houston, Texas

Category C exercises can be summarized as a series of "if-then" scenarios. They include at least two stages of quasi-open-ended choices, with different consequences attached and decisions made and actions taken based on those consequences.

There should be a beginning stage, Stage 1, of at least two choices with different consequences attached. Based on the unique consequence of each choice made from the first decision, at Stage 2 you must (at least) make a second decision that also has unique consequences.

For example, we may pose the question: What tool should we send on the job? Answer options might include Tool A or Tool B. If a learner chooses Tool A, that would lead him or her to answer additional detailed questions based upon that choice of Tool A. Conversely if the learner chooses Tool B, the exercise would lead him or her to an entire other set of follow-up questions based upon Tool B. This cascading tree would continue based upon each question answered.

Figure 7–4 shows the flow of choices and consequences within the two stages.

Figure 7–4. Two Stages of a Category C Exercise

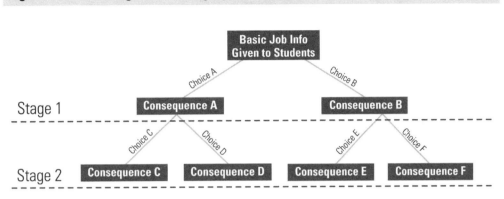

Category C exercises are case study scenarios that are both rewarding and challenging for learners. These exercises are the closest to what is actually done on the job.

One way to develop Category C exercises is by finding old job reports or histories and reverse engineering them. It is also preferable to ask your SME to go step-by-step through the process of solving the exercise.

A downside of these exercises is that they are the most time-consuming to develop. It can be challenging to comb through all your resources to find the information necessary for questions as in-depth as these. Especially when the case study's main functionality is a cause-and-effect, question-and-consequence format, the validity and correctness of your information cannot be fudged. You must make sure all loose ends are tied up.

Another drawback of these exercises is that they take up more class time than others do. Thus, if you are planning for a course to include a Category C activity, make sure there is ample time available.

Basically, Category C exercises are the most involved and challenging ones to complete in class and the most involved and challenging to develop. Still, Category C exercises are an excellent means to help learners apply what they have learned in the classroom to the job.

In summary, there are three categories of exercises. The categories are labeled based on their difficulty to develop and the amount of technical knowledge necessary to create them. Category A exercises are open-ended, generic exercises that could apply to topics across the board and require the least amount of SME input. Category B exercises are generally more controlled, targeted exercises that are specific to a particular topic and require specific answers. Finally, Category C exercises are case scenarios that provide the learner with multiple stages of if-then choices, all leading to different outcomes.

Figure 7–5. Summary of Categories of Exercises

Category of Exercise	Description
Category A	• Easiest to develop. • Knowledge level of learners determines the level of content discussed. • Can be applied to many situations. • Can be vague. • Questions are open-ended. • Relatively quick to develop. • Works well for experienced and highly motivated learners.
Category B	• Targeted questions and exercises. • Cannot be applied word for word to just any topic. • Content and questions are specific to a particular subject. • Takes longer to develop than Category A; less time than Category C. • Ideal for introductory or intermediate courses in which you need to point learners directly to the knowledge you want them to gain. • Often used for targeted, guided training that points learners toward a specific objective and learning outcome.
Category C	• Case studies. • Closest classroom exercise to what is actually done on the job. • Most involved exercise to develop. • Most involved exercise for learners to complete. • Rewarding for learners to complete. • Requires at least two choices to be made based on unique consequences. • Learners are provided different consequences based on the decisions they make during the exercises. Learners must be able to make at least two separate choices.

Building a Library of Examples

Your life as a developer will become easier if you continuously work to build a library of examples of previous exercises you have created. These examples can come in handy when you are trying to describe for your SME something that does not yet exist for the current technical topic. Sometimes it can be difficult for an SME to understand what exactly you are seeking. Instead of simply saying "I need a case study," you can say "I need a case study like this one, but involving your own topic." Showing examples can allow your SME to understand the level of detail you want. Having examples of your work can also help explain what you do at the beginning of a project and can provide an example of what the end product will be.

Creating a library of examples is also helpful in gaining the trust of new SMEs with whom you've never worked and getting them to buy in to the technical design process. (Please review chapter 6 for further explanation.)

Basic Rule

Building a library of exercises (for example, worksheets or case studies) that you have developed helps your SME understand exactly what you are seeking.

Ideas for Exercises

The following are some potential ideas for exercises that you can use in your technical training projects, divided by the three categories outlined previously.

CATEGORY A EXERCISES

What Would You Have Done?

Divide learners into pairs. Ask them to think of a job they have recently accomplished. Ask them to share the descriptions of this job (conditions, location, circumstances, and so on) with their partner and have them ask their partner what he or she would have done if he or she was in the same situation. Let the partners make their guesses and then have the original learners disclose what actually happened on the job. After they have been given ample time to discuss, open the discussions to the class. Ask a few groups to share what they learned.

This exercise gets learners talking about their experiences. It also gets them to think about other alternative actions they could have chosen on the job.

Resource Share

Divide learners into groups. Ask them to come up with a list of all the resources they currently use to do their jobs, including electronic files, computer programs, personalized spreadsheets, books, manuals, cheat sheets, handbooks, brochures, websites, and so on. Have each group present its list to the rest of the class and explain where each of these resources can be found. Encourage learners to share their own resources with others. Provide a prize to the group that provides the rest of the class with the most resources.

This exercise is good for allowing learners to share the location of resources related to the job.

Job Aid Lecture Break

After the instructor gives a lecture, stop and give the participants 10 minutes to make a job aid based on what they see as relevant material that will help them to do their jobs better.

This simple exercise allows learners to specifically apply material covered in class to the job.

Lead the Blind

Divide learners into pairs. In each pair, blindfold one learner and have the other lead the first one to different products placed around the room. The blindfolded learner must describe out loud what he or she feels (for example, here is a smooth, concave object, and so forth) and then ask questions to determine what the product is. The pair moves on to the next tool after the blindfolded learner identifies the product. You can space the products around the room, and when the partners get about halfway, you can have them switch the blindfold.

This exercise is good for physical, tactile learners who enjoy being actively involved and using their hands.

CATEGORY B EXERCISES

Piece of the Puzzle

Enlarge a picture of a system. Cut out the different components. Give each learner a component of the system, and then ask the learners to get together to arrange all of their pieces together in order to build the system. After the class has "built" the system, ask each participant to explain what role his or her particular component plays in the entire process.

This exercise is good for instances when participants need to learn the process of a system, or how a piece of equipment functions internally.

Explain the Assembly

Pass out sample product or tool assembly drawings to each group. Instruct the learners to

- explain the use of the assembly
- label the individual components shown on the assembly drawing and explain how the individual components function
- circle any weak points in the configuration and give their rationale for these choices.

Have the learners give a group presentation to the rest of the class when they are finished. Discuss the results.

This exercise allows learners to discuss the internal components and functioning of a technical product.

Right and Wrong Assemblies

Divide learners into groups, and pass out three or more assembly drawings to each group. At least one assembly drawing should be incorrect. Ask the learners to analyze the drawings and determine which ones are correct and which ones are not. They will have to explain their rationale.

This exercise is good for helping participants learn about the internal functioning of a product as well as for providing a platform to practice catching common errors.

Design Your Own Equipment

Give your learners a hypothetical job scenario. Ask them to design their own tool or system to meet the needs of the job. The only caveat is that they cannot use any existing equipment the company has or any that they know a competitor has. Ask the learners to come up with a picture of their design as well as a basic description of how the design works. During discussion, ask learners to relate the functionality of their made-up equipment to the functionality of equipment the company actually carries.

This exercise allows learners to think about what is possible, as well as to see where existing equipment is useful.

CATEGORY C EXERCISES

Case Scenario

Divide learners into groups and provide them with a list of job characteristics. (If possible, give this information on the actual platform—for example, job order forms—that learners use on the job.) Ask the groups to choose equipment for that scenario. Have them present their equipment choices to you, the "customer." Based on the information they give you, either accept the equipment choices or change the equipment slightly. As a second part of this exercise, based on the equipment selected, learners must create a running procedure. As a final step of the case scenario, give groups a specific description of something that has gone wrong on their job, based on their equipment and running procedure. Learners must identify why this mistake occurred and what to do to fix it. Groups should share their answers with the class.

This exercise is a good way to simulate the steps and the decisions that learners are likely to face on the job.

Taking a Critical Look at Exercises

There will be times in your course development that you come across a complex technical topic that, upon asking your SME a few questions, suddenly becomes very clear to you! This is exciting for you, and in your exuberance, you may decide that this particular point is one that should have an extensive exercise in your course because it made the topic so much clearer to you and it will be the secret ticket to understanding the subject and . . . slow down. Before running off and adding a half day to the course to incorporate your newfound understanding into course exercises, make sure that you double-check with your SME that the point is one most people find difficult to understand, and that the concept is truly one that's important to the course.

Although you, as a person with a novice understanding of the technical topic, may find this nugget of information to be perfect for your course, it may be akin to teaching basic arithmetic to an audience of astrophysicists.

It doesn't matter how good your newfound exercise might be; if most people already understand the concept or the concept is not that important to the course, then not much time needs to be spent on it. You must be able to accept this.

Basic Rule

Exercises should be included only if they help the target audience meet the course objectives.

Noted

If the target audience members are identified as novices, you may have a case to keep your exercise. The things that don't make sense to you probably won't make sense to other novices learning them. However, if the audience is experienced and your SME does not think the exercise is useful, there is a good chance you will have to tone down your enthusiasm and let go of your plans.

Getting It Done

Sound instructional principles still apply even when a topic is highly technical. This is the basic mantra of technical training design. New teaching strategies have replaced "the 100 percent lecture course." Although your SME might be accustomed to simple lecture plus PowerPoint, this is not the most effective style of training. A complicated topic does not mean that it is OK for the instruction to include only a PowerPoint lecture. As we learned with the primacy-recency effect, lectures should be broken apart in order to maximize retention. There are a variety of exercises that can be included in the class that can function to support course objectives and to break up the lecture.

Exercises can take a number of forms, from the generic Category A exercise to the specific Category B exercise to the involved Category C exercise. It is important that you begin to build a library of examples so that you can better explain to your SME what you want. While there are a variety of exercises that you can incorporate into your class, you still need to keep the objectives of the course in mind. If an exercise does not help to meet a course objective, it is not needed in the training class.

In summary, incorporating a variety of useful, relevant, and challenging exercises increases the value of technical training.

Worksheet 7–1. Sample Category A Exercise

The following is a Category A worksheet that could more or less apply to most technical topics. You can use this example as an exercise for your course.

Contingencies		
Analyze your job. Describe what can go wrong on a job, why this can happen, and possible options to fix the problem.		
What can go wrong	Why this happens	How to fix it

Worksheet 7–2. Sample Category C Exercise

The following is a worksheet that you can use to create a Categorgy C exercise for your course.

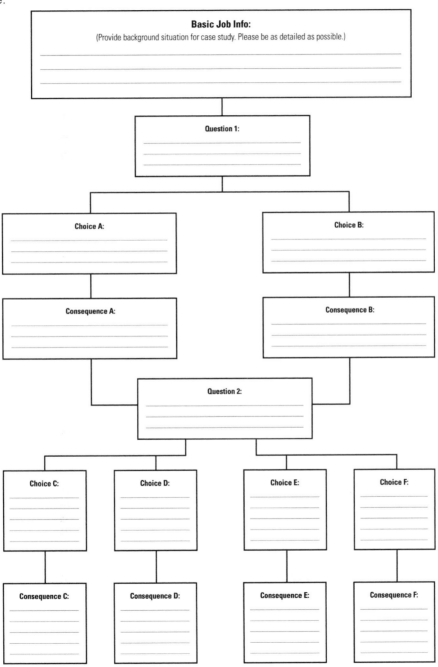

8

The Pilot Class and Beyond

What's Inside This Chapter

In this chapter, you'll learn

▶ how to help out the SME-turned-trainer
▶ development opportunities from the pilot class
▶ postcourse maintenance.

At this point, your course has been accepted, and you've made it to the pilot class stage. As happy as you may be, your job is not quite done. You need to first be able to effectively transfer the project to the instructor of the course, and then you need to observe and analyze the course in action to determine whether your objectives and design are sound. In addition, you should put some steps in place so that your material can be more easily updated and kept relevant. These items will be discussed in this chapter.

Helping Out the SME-Turned-Trainer

Typically, subject matter experts (SMEs) also double as instructors of technical training classes. While there are rare times when a complete nonexpert teaches a technical topic or when an SME is permanently paired with someone who specializes in classroom instruction, you will find these to be the exceptions, rather than the rule. Most of the time, an SME will instruct the class him- or herself. As such, there are certain things you can do to help out the SME-turned-trainer both before and during the pilot class.

Course "Dry Run" Before the Pilot

You can help out the SME-turned-trainer by having a run-through of the course materials before the pilot class. Explain the rationale of the organizational structure, the exercises, and any other particulars of the class. If possible, have the instructor practice the presentation or complete portions of the exercises him- or herself.

Basic Rule

You need to brief the SME-turned-trainer on the course content before the pilot class.

You should go over course content verbally with the SME-turned-trainer, but you might also consider having an instructor's guide printed out. Creating an instructor's guide can really help ensure that your course will continue to be delivered as originally designed and developed. This instructor's guide can be as simple as a one-page typed schedule, or it can be as detailed as a full-blown facilitator's guide with descriptions, rationale and answers to exercises, notes included for the PowerPoint slides, and so on.

The course dry run is also a good time to review adult learning principles. If your instructor seems hesitant about interactivity or any of the other instructionally related features of the course, you might provide resources that prove that adult learning principles are tested and sound. It can ease your instructor's mind if you explain that you will be there to assist in the class (for example, by helping to explain exercise instructions or to provide guidance in keeping the course on track). This not only can help calm your instructor's nerves about trying something new, but will prepare the instructor for you to stand up and help out during the class.

Resist any urges to change material—unless it is incorrect—at this stage if the pilot class will be happening sooner than would allow for completion of the requested changes. Ask the SME to give the course a try as it is and then explain that you'll be open to removing anything that doesn't work *after* the pilot.

Noted

The pilot class can give you an opportunity to demonstrate a great new exercise or technique to your instructors.

One time, I worked on developing a new introductory course for the oil services industry. The instructor was very experienced and knowledgeable, but was stuck in a slide show lecture rut. I designed a fun, hands-on exercise that required the learners to work in groups using basic craft supplies to create a simple oil field tool called a "Poor Boy" basket or finger basket. As this type of exercise was way outside of my instructor's comfort zone, he fought against its inclusion in the class, but grudgingly allowed me to demonstrate it during the pilot class.

Well, the learners loved the exercise! They thought that it enhanced their understanding of the tool and that it gave them a fun way to break up the monotony of the afternoon lecture. Once my instructor saw the success of this exercise during the pilot class, he became much more receptive to my ideas for other classes.

—Stefanie Matta, Contract Technical Writer, Houston, Texas

Assistance During the Class

Don't be afraid to stand up and help out the instructor during the pilot course. Think of yourself as a co-facilitator, especially when it comes time to explain the instructions for participant exercises. If you notice the instructor getting completely off track, ask if the class can have a break and privately discuss this with the instructor.

Noted

Sometimes instructors will be nervous to have someone in their class observing them. Be conscientious about not appearing as a judge or critic.

If you have to jump in to help, it will usually be when the exercises occur. Flag the exercises the instructor has trouble with during the pilot. Make a note to add additional detailed written instructions and possibly even a sample completed problem and answer for the learners to view before completing the exercise themselves. These types of things can augment some of the instructor's verbal directions.

In addition, you may need to rethink whether to include certain kinds of exercises in the course. You may have created the best exercise ever, but if the instructor doesn't use it, the exercise will not be effective. The intricacies and detail included in administrating the exercises you design should match the facilitation skills of the instructor. Some instructors just may not have the skills or motivation to try an exercise with a lot of steps. In that case, the exercise may need to be replaced with something else.

Approach instructor tangents just as you did when developing and gathering material with your SME: warily, but with some leeway available. Sometimes tangents occur because the instructor has noticed a hole in the content and that a new objective is necessary. Sometimes instructor tangents are OK—they may answer learners' questions and aid in their understanding. It will be up to you to determine whether the tangents are ambling mindlessly or are fit-for-purpose.

Effectively briefing and supporting the SME-turned-trainer is just one aspect of the pilot class. The next section will discuss development opportunities from the pilot class.

Development Opportunities from the Pilot Class

During the pilot course, both you and the instructor should be analyzing whether

- ▶ course objectives are met through the training content provided
- ▶ there is a logical flow of material
- ▶ technical explanations are complete
- ▶ unnecessary information is removed
- ▶ course exercises are challenging, useful, and relevant.

Attendees in the course can be great sources to help you determine whether the conditions listed above describe your course. Attendees can be polled or pre- and post-tested to determine whether your course objectives really are on track and whether your design of material actually helps to meet course objectives.

When considering input, you have a couple of choices for the pilot class: You can tell the learners the course is a pilot run, or you can avoid letting on to anyone that this is the first time that this course has been taught.

Option 1: Tell the Learners It Is a Pilot Run

Sometimes, if a course is highly anticipated, it will be next to impossible to keep it a secret that this is the first time it has been run. In addition, many instructors choose to explain to learners that the course is a pilot run because those instructors are not confident with the material, so saying it is a pilot serves as a disclaimer that makes the instructors feel better and above potential criticism.

A benefit of sharing that it is a pilot class is that you can request feedback and hold periodic open and honest discussions about whether course content is effective and working. You are basically attempting to enlist the learners as co-creators and trying to make them feel invested in the outcome of the course. If you are able to achieve this, learners' feedback will be especially valuable.

A possible drawback of this is that the learners may not be as objective with their comments and evaluations; they may be more forgiving because they may not think the content is "final."

Option 2: Don't Let On That It Is a Pilot Course

This allows you to get more objective reactions of course content from learners. You get to see what their reactions would be if the content presented was the finalized version, including what portions learners like and what portions may need more work. Of course, you will probably already have ideas about these things, but the feedback is still quite valuable and more "pure." Often, you will be surprised with at least some aspects of what learners thought was effective or not effective.

Regardless of which route you choose, it is important that you tap into learners' reactions during the pilot course. This will give you a chance to see how learners respond to the material, both positively and negatively. Keep an eye out during the class to see where they struggle and where they are not engaged. You can document questions learners have and different content areas that appear difficult to understand. Don't be afraid to ask the learners directly for feedback. Speaking to the target audience firsthand can help you to figure out what works and what does not, and which objectives are needed and which are not. You will probably find that the learners have good suggestions for activities and content, and many will even possess hidden gems of relevant technical information.

As the pilot class proceeds, you should be analyzing objectives, content, areas for interactivity, learners' reactions, their questions, and extra things the instructor says (things not mentioned in the presentation or the materials). Below are specific items to consider when sitting through a pilot class:

- Are learners engaged in all sections of the course? Is there something we could add to further engage learners?
- Does the target audience feel all objectives were met? That all objectives were necessary? That any important objectives were missing?
- Do learners express positive ratings or comments about the course structure and content?
- In which areas of the course did learners have a lot of questions? Were these questions answered by the current course material?
- What new explanations did the instructor include as the class occurred? Do those explanations need to be formally included in the content?
- Did learners find any inconsistencies or mistakes in the material?
- Did learners reference other resources that might be useful to include in the course?
- Are there any areas in which we can include a more complete or more updated example in the material?
- Are there any ways we can make the learners more responsible for their own learning?
- Do we make any general statements or assumptions in the material that are confusing to learners? How should we adjust the text, or what specific examples can we include?

From the information you gather from the pilot class, you should be able to make one more major update and then be done with your course (or at least be done with the first version of it!).

Other Opportunities from the Pilot

There is nothing like a pilot class to find the final pieces of missing information you need. For example, in pilot classes you could do the following:

- Give learners exercises to complete that—despite your best efforts—you were not able to get answers for yet. In cases in which you have extreme trouble getting answers, it is possible you will attain these answers from learners during the pilot. After they complete the exercise and share their answers, you can document the correct input and make these answers part of the permanent instructor's guide.

▶ Ask learners in the pilot course to create questions for a needed final exam. At the end of the class, divide the learners into groups and assign each group a course objective. Ask learners to create five test questions based on what they have learned about their assigned course objective. For the pilot class, you can use these questions as a trivia game, which temporarily functions as the final exam. After the pilot, however, you should be able to use these test questions as a starting point for creating a permanent written exam for the next class.

These examples are a little scrappy, but sometimes measures like this are necessary. You can use the pilot as a way to finally find the rest of the technical information you are seeking for a course. It should be noted—importantly—that *if you are going the route of an unfinished or unpolished pilot course, you must be aware of how you advertise the course, who attends, and what kind of "course credit" you give!*

After you have updated your course accordingly based on the pilot class, your next step will be saying good-bye to your course for good . . . or at least for a little while.

Postcourse Maintenance

It is important to keep your course updated and relevant; yet it is also important that you be able to say "good-bye" to a project so that you can move on to your next priority. Postcourse maintenance can be a tricky thing, but there are measures you can take in order to keep a project "closed" for an appropriate amount of time, while still providing updated content to the learners.

Dealing with "Tweaks" in Material

It can be next to impossible to get your course absolutely perfect. Your SME (or you) will probably want to make a tweak here or there. Constantly opening and closing a project for small details, however, can be a major disruption in your work process and efficiencies.

You can meet this "tweak" challenge by logging all the small changes needed for a course and then waiting to deal with them until enough have built up to validate a major overhaul of the course. For example, as your instructor continues to teach the course, provide a worksheet for your instructor to log any improvements he or she thinks could be made. Set up an electronic file in which the instructor can enter new information and requested changes. Keep this information as long-term data to be incorporated into the next major redevelopment of the course.

Basically, you should set up a location for the instructor to keep track of eventual changes he or she wants made, and then periodically return to the class once enough major changes to the material are needed—that is, when enough changes are needed to justify reopening the project.

Keeping Content Updated

It is important that technical content stay up-to-date. One suggestion is to provide your instructor with a sample "addendum" worksheet template, so that he or she can list additional important updates, changes, and so on that come up and give this addendum worksheet to learners along with the "regular" course materials. This allows the instructor some control over keeping the content up-to-date, and it also prevents you from having to jump at every minor edit.

Noted

"It's not you, it's me."
If you have been effective in establishing a partnership with your SME, it can be especially difficult for your SME to understand that you have "closed" the project. In some cases the SME may feel disappointed or let down that you are no longer actively working on the course. If this is the case for you, first of all, cheer up! If the SME misses you on the project, this indicates that you must have done a good job and that you were successful in establishing a team atmosphere. Second, you can ease the pains for your SME by explaining that it is nothing personal toward him or her or the project, but rather, it is your own workload that necessitates the closure. Assuring your SME that steps are in place to keep track of eventual updates can help as well.

Getting It Done

As happy as you may be to have made it to the pilot course stage, your job is not done. You need to first be able to transfer the project to the instructor of the course, and then you need to observe the course in action to determine that your objectives and design are sound and relevant. The pilot course is an opportunity to test your development project. As the pilot class proceeds, you should be analyzing objectives, content, areas for interactivity, learners' reactions, their questions, and extra things the instructor says. In addition, you should put some steps in place so that your material can be more easily updated and kept relevant.

Saying good-bye to technical training projects should be a happy event; from this day forward, you will have successfully provided the organization with a useful and relevant training course that can assist employee performance.

Worksheet 8–1. Pilot Course Evaluation—Developer and Instructor

Use the following worksheet to evaluate the pilot course. You can ask your instructor/SME to fill out the worksheet as well.

Based on the Pilot Course

Objectives are
- ☐ appropriate to the target audience
- ☐ relevant to the organization and business strategy
- ☐ specific, measurable, achievable, realistic, and testable.

Information is
- ☐ complete
- ☐ accurate
- ☐ concise.

Exercises
- ☐ meet course objectives
- ☐ engage learners
- ☐ include clear instructions
- ☐ are easy to administer.

In regard to course structure,
- ☐ overall organization of the course works
- ☐ flow of each section makes sense
- ☐ length of the course is appropriate
- ☐ level of content is appropriate.

Additional comments:

Worksheet 8–2. Pilot Course Evaluation—Learner

Hand out the following worksheet to learners after your pilot course in order to help you gauge learner reaction and capture learner comments. Adjust the worksheet as necessary to meet your own specific needs.

Please rate your knowledge level before attending the course.

Novice   Expert

   1   2   3   4   5

Please rate your knowledge level after attending the course.

Novice   Expert

   1   2   3   4   5

Course materials are organized and easy to follow.

Strongly Disagree   Disagree   Neutral   Agree   Strongly Agree

Course exercises helped me learn the content.

Strongly Disagree   Disagree   Neutral   Agree   Strongly Agree

The course will help me do my job better.

Strongly Disagree   Disagree   Neutral   Agree   Strongly Agree

Comments:

What did you like about the course?

How could the course be improved?

Would you recommend this course to others?

Worksheet 8–3. Sample "Updates to Content" Worksheet

The following is an example of a worksheet that you can give to your instructor/SME in order to allow him or her to provide learners with updated information related to course content that has not yet been formally incorporated in the course materials.

As you know, technology is always changing. Please note the following updates to the course material. Thank you.

Section 1

_____

_____

_____

_____

_____

Section 2

_____

_____

_____

_____

Section 3

_____

_____

_____

_____

Additional comments:

_____

_____

_____

_____

_____

9

Troubleshooting: Challenges and Solutions

What's Inside This Chapter

In this chapter, you'll learn

▶ descriptions of technical training development challenges and potential solutions

▶ a final word on technical training development.

By now you have made your way through almost this entire book; however, that does not mean that your future as a perfect technical training developer is certain. Technical training development is not an easy job. Technical training is a field that is fraught with challenges, some of which you may never anticipate.

Challenges are not impossibilities, though. They are opportunities: chances to display your perseverance, your creativity, and your ability to troubleshoot; to face issues, analyze them, and work through them. This chapter discusses potential technical training challenges and gives examples of potential solutions. Note that the solutions offered are not exhaustive. This chapter is designed to get you started. You should be able to continue to come up with more solutions that meet your needs.

Challenge: Technical Content Is Too Complicated

Most every technical training developer has had the experience of feeling completely clueless when listening to a room full of subject matter experts (SMEs). It is normal for a new developer to not fully understand the jargon and complex concepts involved in a new technical topic. Most technical topics have their own language: distinct names, acronyms, principles, and so on. Learning this technical language can take time.

Potential solutions for this quite common challenge include the following:

Learn as much as you can. This sounds obvious, but asking as many questions as you can, and reading as much information as you can find, will eventually help. By no means are you to become an expert (that's why we have SMEs), but learning enough that you can speak somewhat intelligently about the subject with your SME makes for a much easier project.

Make your own dictionary. One thing you can do to help keep yourself organized (and sane) is to keep a list of relevant technical terms and acronyms you have learned. This way you will have a quick reference sheet as you go through the development process.

Try it out. Don't underestimate the power of seeing for yourself. See if you can try out the task or touch the product yourself. If you are able to go out to the lab, the shop, the field, the operating room, and so on, you can get a firsthand look at your technical topic. This experience can be invaluable as you gather information and develop your course.

Noted

I cannot stress the "try it out" suggestion enough in the instructional developer's effort to create effective technical training. During a recent manufacturing tour, it was amazing to hear training development staff remark how different a product appeared in reality versus graphically. Lightbulbs began to turn on among the staff, which increased the quality of our deliverables. Though you may not always be allowed to experience or see the product or task you are describing, make every effort with the assistance of your SME to obtain this critical base for your knowledge.

—Patty Murdock, Technical Training Manager, Schlumberger, Houston, Texas

Tie the topic to a job or a task whenever possible. Sometimes discussing a highly technical topic within the context of the job or the "real world" can make it seem more approachable and understandable. Even with complicated topics, a good SME should be able to walk you through the basic process of the job and pinpoint major portions that should be clarified and emphasized.

Ask for analogies. Ask your SME if he or she can rephrase complex technical descriptions or give you an analogy. This solution comes from the old television show *Star Trek*. Often in the show, the crew of the *Enterprise* faces some bizarre space anomaly too complex to put into words suitable for a standard television audience, so the writers simplify the anomaly into something that people can visualize. For example, consider which statement is easier to visualize: "The *Enterprise* is to travel at precisely warp 4.3 on the specific trajectory equidistant from all boundaries of a globular cluster's outer rim" or "It's like threading a needle in space."

Similarly, if your SME can give you an analogy or rephrase complex issues into something more easily recognizable for you, this can demystify the "technobabble" and make it easier to grasp the complicated stuff.

Challenge: You Can't Tell What Content Is "Nice to Know" and What Is "Need to Know"

If you are not deeply familiar with the topic at hand, it can be difficult to determine what technical content is "nice to know" and what content is "need to know." As a developer, though, you will have to function as a filter and ensure that the material included really is related to the objectives of the course.

Sometimes there is a relative scarcity in text regarding technical products or tasks. When a developer does find a hidden cache of content, there is the temptation to use it, even if it diverts the learners too far away from the main objective of the module.

Solutions for this challenge include the following:

Stay disciplined. An overarching solution to this challenge is that you must always stay disciplined with your content. If you fill your classes with filler, you will lose your participants' attention. It sometimes happens that you will find a bit of training that is clearly understandable and fun to teach, but if it diverts you from your objectives, you must refrain from including it. You must have the discipline to stay on your prescribed task and not be self-indulgent with your topics. In technical training, brevity is a virture. Keep the self-control to get rid of content that is not related to the objectives of the section.

Question your SME. If you suspect your SME is veering off in a wayward direction with the course content (a direction that does not match previously agreed-on objectives) quiz him or her about it. Asking "How does this help meet our course objectives?" is a simple way for you to figure out how the information fits. If the information does not fit nicely, ask why. Course objectives were set at the beginning of the project for a reason: The objectives were labeled as priorities. Don't be afraid to question why course content differs from objectives.

Noted

There will be times that you find you do need to amend the objectives. This is fine, as long as there is a clear business case that supports this change.

Believe your SME. As you are not the expert on the content, there will be times that you need to bite your tongue and simply take your SME's word for it. It is possible that seemingly "wayward" course content is applicable to the course objectives, but you just can't see it because of your own lack of understanding of the concept. While you should strive to keep to your previously agreed-on objectives, you also shouldn't be a slave to them—it is possible that objectives may change slightly as you get deeper into the material and your SME realizes that certain facts were originally overlooked. If this is the case, you will just have to trust your SME.

Challenge: Your SME Has a Full-time Job Outside of the Training Department

In a perfect world, the sole priority of your SME would be to finish your training course. Unfortunately, there will be times that you will be paired with an SME who already has a full-time job outside of developing your course.

In these instances, obviously, your SME will have other things competing for his or her time. This can result in strained communication between you and your SME, slow progression on your project, and even missed deadlines.

There are a few solutions for this challenge:

Ask for management support. If your SME has many things competing for his or her attention, an obvious solution is to ask for management support for your SME to make your project his or her number-one priority.

Set realistic timelines. Always keep in mind that your SME has another job—probably one that he or she enjoys. Be sure that you honor your SME's obligations and set reasonable timelines that work for both of you.

Spread the work around. In the event that your SME simply cannot provide you with enough time, you must arrange for a few other SMEs to share the burden. Often, management will be happy to point you in the direction of other specialists who can help. This way, your needs are fulfilled, and the burden is not placed on any one person.

Challenge: The Course You Have Been Asked to Redesign Has Already Been Taught for Years

Being tasked to redesign a course that's been in place for a while can be a positive or a negative thing. The good news about this challenge is that content is likely to be available and easily accessible for your technical subject. The bad news is that if the content is bad, sometimes it can be especially hard to convince your SME to abandon that content completely. After an SME/instructor has been teaching the same class for a long time, materials tend to become "cemented," and it can be harder to go back and change. Your SME/instructor may think: "Hey, my class works fine. I did this for years. I like it." In this situation, you might have a more challenging time "selling" a different course structure because something else is already established.

If bad news is the case for you, you might try the following solutions:

Sit through the existing class. If you are able, it can be very helpful to sit through the old class before you start your redesign. The benefit is that you can get a feel for the subject matter and learn about it as you observe. You can see firsthand what works and what doesn't. As you observe, you can start to piece together the objectives of the current material and use them as a starting point for the "formal" development of the redesign. In addition, if a total overhaul of the entire course structure is necessary, you will have built some credibility for your case by at least seeing what the old structure was like.

Don't appear overly critical or judgmental. Someone spent a great deal of time putting this course together initially, which means someone is probably going to be attached to all—or parts—of the course. Tread carefully so that you don't offend or alienate someone who could possibly provide updated, good information for the redesigned class.

Noted

I think clarifying purpose is another method to help convince an SME/instructor to loosen his or her grip on legacy material. Contemporary technical instruction should be replicable, deliver verifiable value to the revenue-producing segments, and be translatable (if it is a global operation), auditable, teachable, and understandable to the target audience. Anything less is a waste of time and money to the corporation.

—Kenny Amend, Area Manager, Weatherford International, Houston, Texas

Challenge: The Course That Never Gets Finished

At one time or another, most of us have experienced the bane of the developer's existence: The Course That Never Gets Finished. The Course That Never Gets Finished is that class that you seem to be endlessly working on—and off—and on—for what seems like an eternity. It is disruptive, and it is maddening.

There could be multiple reasons that a perfectly good course turns into The Course That Never Gets Finished. These reasons might include

- ▶ unclear expectations
- ▶ unavailable information
- ▶ overzealous objectives
- ▶ poor project management
- ▶ changing priorities by the organization.

Here are some solutions to this exceptionally annoying challenge:

Correctly pinpoint the issues. You can create all the solutions in the world, but if you do not take a good hard look at why a perfectly good course has turned into The Course That Never Gets Finished, you will end up spinning your wheels. You need to be able to pinpoint correctly the issues involved: Is this an "information" problem? Is this an SME issue? Does the SME understand what is asked of him or her? Was the project never that critical to the organization? Does the project just need to be scrapped? Does the project need to be reworked so that it is critical? Does the project have proper stakeholders identified, and does it have the management support needed to push it along?

Get organized. Document exactly what on the project is complete, and what still needs to be completed. In addition, assign responsibilities for who is to complete each unfinished task. Place a date on this document and store it in an easily accessible location.

Make things as clear as possible for your SME. If you find yourself in a situation in which an SME never completes his or her tasks on time, you will need to take a closer look at the situation. Sometimes, SMEs do not get things done in a timely fashion—or on our time schedules—because they are unclear about what we are really asking of them. They simply don't have a full understanding of what we are seeking or how to do what we are asking. Remember, as foreign as the technical content is to you, often course development is just as foreign to an SME. Show the SME examples of past work so it is very clear what you are asking. And finally, it never hurts to show the SME understanding and patience.

Get help. Try to secure additional SMEs or developers to finish compiling material and develop the course. Sometimes if a project has been sitting vacant for a while it is because the tasks associated with completing it are too daunting. Spreading the work around can help.

Consider scaling back the objectives. A project sitting unfinished can also indicate that perhaps your original course objectives were overzealous. You may need to return to your initial needs analysis and reanalyze. If the missing information is still necessary, you might consider modularizing the course. This way, the "finished material" can still be taught and used as long as the unfinished material continues to be "unfinished."

Redefine timetables. As so much of what we do is dependent on other people, it is difficult to estimate how long things will take. When projecting completion dates for technical training, if possible, forecast your estimates to reflect the amount of time it will take you to finish *after* you get the last item of requested information.

For example, Kristine, the boss, asks Technical Developer Will when the course will be finished. Will, who is still waiting on information from Subject Matter Expert Marty, wisely responds, "It will be done exactly five days after Marty gets me that last bit of information."

You may have little control over when your SMEs will give you information, so if you base your estimate on what you think your SMEs should do, when they don't do it, you are suddenly the one who cannot meet deadlines. Therefore, if possible, try to word and structure your deadlines so that you are estimating just the things you have direct control over: the content after you receive it in full.

Hold a pilot course. Sometimes actually going ahead and setting a pilot course date can speed things along and force the technical training project to become a higher priority. Of course, if you go this route, you should be prepared to hold the course even if you are not fully ready. (The previous chapter in this book offers additional information about pilot courses.)

Get management buy-in. This is short and simple: Either get management buy-in or lose the class for good.

Challenge: The Course That Needs to Be Finished Yesterday

Most all developers have been there. A training request comes in. You look it over; it seems reasonable and doable. So far, so good, but then comes the bomb: The course must be finished in exactly three days or else! I introduce . . . The Course That Needs to Be Finished Yesterday. Whether this particular challenge arises from rapidly changing technology or unrealistic development expectations from the organization, a course that needs to be developed without adequate development time allotted can cause major headaches.

Noted

Training is not a "drive thru" event, where you order training at one window and pick it up at the next.

—Bob Taylor, Founder, Taylormade Training Consultants, Perth, Australia

In situations in which you are faced with unrealistic time constraints, there are a few solutions from which you can choose:

Educate the organization. When dealt an unpractical course development deadline, it is necessary to explain adequately to the organization the course development process and, most specifically, the benefits of each step of the process. Point out to the organization the long-term risks of not spending adequate development time on a technical training project. Use this discussion to redefine timetables into something more doable for you.

Get help. If management has designated this course as a high priority and it is necessary that the course be finished immediately, get help to finish the project. Leverage the importance of the course in order to secure additional SMEs and developers to finish it.

Focus on the most important objective. If a project needs to be rolled out immediately, take a critical look at the most important objective, and spend the bulk of your available time making sure that it is covered well. Most people would agree: It is better to do one thing well than a dozen things terribly.

Use the pilot course. If you are pressed for time and technical content but the show must go on, use the pilot course as one of your information-gathering strategies. After you have created a solid design document, task the participants in the pilot with supplying the needed information from the design document as part of the requirements of the first course. This will mean that the participants in the pilot are getting a slightly different transfer of information and means of instruction, but at least the material is being taught and the course is moving forward. The first pilot course will essentially function as your "soft opening," but from there, as you gather information, each class should become more and more complete.

Challenge: The Organization Doesn't Understand Active Training

It is no secret that active learning is necessary to achieve acceptable adult learning and retention levels. Yet many organizations fail to use these principles in their technical classroom training. One reason may be that people are not aware of existing research and have been content with the status quo of just "telling" the learners what they need to know through a lecture. Another reason may be that it is simply more challenging to develop interactive technical training based on the complexity of the subject matter.

If all the organization expects from you is a PowerPoint presentation and a final exam, you have a dilemma: Do you give the organization "just a PowerPoint," or do you actually provide the organization with a quality product—a training course that takes into account instructional design and adult learning principles?

Hopefully you will be able to prevail with an active classroom. Here are a few things you can do to help convince the organization:

Reference the research. Scientific minds respect scientific research. There exists valid scientifically tested learning and memory research. Do your homework and present this information to your organization, whether verbally, in a PowerPoint, in a formal course, or as a handout.

Noted

Traditionally, organizations that use technical training most often are not the welcoming adopters of interactive adult learning principles. The direct lecture method is viewed as the only "true" training model, and interactivity is considered a tool for children. If you work within an organization, consider developing a "Train the Trainer" course, which models interactive learning. You will be amazed at the progress a trainer makes toward understanding and utilizing the interactive model. I knew it had impact when an experienced trainer sheepishly admitted that he realized the concepts we continually discuss in course development meetings truly work in the adult classroom. Using a "Train the Trainer" course as a comprehensive explanation of proven techniques and methods has made a dramatic difference in the quality and usage of adult learning principles in our organization.

—Patty Murdock, Technical Training Manager, Schlumberger, Houston, Texas

Show a previous project. Sometimes it is helpful to show a finished product before you begin. Previous courses you designed, as well as positive comments from participants who went through previous courses you developed, can help the tentative organization see that active training can be beneficial and successful.

Keep it simple. When in doubt, keep the exercises simple. Take baby steps incorporating interactivity. Include transition slides from the lecture to the activity so that the instructor can more easily make a smooth transition from passive to active learning. Do not design highly involved exercises that are complicated to administer. Make the exercises straightforward and simple. Then, as the organization gets used to the idea of basic activities and interactivity, you can get more daring with your exercises.

Challenge: You Don't Know How to Make the Content Interactive

For whatever reason, when subjects are highly technical, it can be more challenging to build interactivity into a classroom course.

Solutions to this problem include the following:

Enlist your SME. It is extremely helpful if you can enlist your SME to help think up ways to make a particular section interactive. If you can get your SME to understand what you are after, the SME's intimate knowledge of the topic can add ingenuity, as well as breadth and depth, to the exercises that you might not have been able to generate on your own.

Again, keep it simple. There are a variety of Category A training exercises that can be used for most classes. You do not have to develop intricate games and exercises for all of your training courses. You can still be effective with simple worksheets and learner discussions.

Challenge: SMEs Disagree on Content

It is no fun being in the middle of disagreeing SMEs. Besides holding up the project, disagreeing SMEs can make you uncomfortable on a personal level if you are forced to choose sides and pick one SME's content over another's.

This challenge can be tricky, but possible solutions include the following:

Bring 'em in. Gather all of the disagreeing SMEs, put them in a room together, and let them figure out what the final content should be. This takes your personal preferences out of the situation, and it lets the experts decide.

Ask management. If your SMEs have reached an impasse, you can enlist management to make the final call on content.

Include multiple perspectives in the content. If your topic truly has no absolute right or wrong answers, your SMEs have agreed to disagree, and management doesn't want to make the call, it is OK to include multiple perspectives in the content. If handled correctly, these sometimes contentious areas can make good group discussions and exercises. For example, you might assign each group a different perspective and ask the groups to come up with an argument for their assigned perspective. Then you can let the groups debate with each other. This encourages dialogue and lets learners know that multiple perspectives exist in a particular area.

Challenge: Equipment Is Unavailable for Training

In an ideal world, we would have all of the necessary equipment and infrastructure to make the training environment perfectly mimic the job. Unfortunately, this is not always the case. For various reasons, sometimes equipment is simply not available for training. You are left essentially "trying to teach someone to swim without a swimming pool."

If this is the case, there are a few things you can do:

Talk to management. Explain the issue to management and see if you can gain some support for providing the equipment for training courses. Have a plan ready for exactly what you want, why it is necessary, and how much it will cost. And then . . . be persuasive.

Use media. If equipment is not available, media can be the next best thing. Use as many pictures, videos, and animations as you can get your hands on.

Create on-the-job training. If course-essential equipment is not available, you may need to rethink whether a classroom course is really the best choice for the situation. Consider whether the classroom course could be converted to on-the-job training if you were to simply provide some formalized resources. If aspects of the technical content require a classroom course, but you still absolutely need the equipment as well, you might consider holding the classroom portion for theory and then creating an on-the-job follow-up self-study as an accompaniment for the classroom course.

Challenge: Concrete Answers Do Not Exist

It can be a challenge if your technical topic is not an exact science and concrete answers do not exist for your content.

In these situations, you can do the following:

Assess the situation. It is *very* important that you determine whether concrete answers truly do not exist or simply that your SME does not know what the correct answer is.

Noted

When a question is identified for you as something that does not have one correct answer, sometimes this is a matter of your SME not knowing whether something is verified or whether he or she is authorized to make a particular decision. If you suspect this is the case, the only way of knowing is to simply ask a few follow-up questions with your SME.

—Kenny Amend, Area Manager, Weatherford International, Houston, Texas

In addition, there are some safety- and health-related items that require absolute concrete answers. If this is the case for your technical topic, it is extremely important that you be diligent and find the correct and complete answers to your questions.

Beware of using absolutes. You need to make sure that when you write your materials you are careful about what you claim through your wording. Instead of using absolutes such as "always" and "never," you should default to using "often" and "sometimes" unless an absolute is specifically requested by the SME.

Here are some examples:

Absolute: Widgets are always used in these situations.

Indirectly Absolute: Widgets are used in these situations.

Better: Widgets are often used in these situations.

Better: Widgets are sometimes used in these situations.

Noted

Again, it is important that you determine whether concrete answers truly do not exist or that your SME simply does not know what the correct answer is.

Use an educated guess. And then recognize that other alternatives exist. Sometimes you just need to make your best guess on which answer to feature, and then formally recognize within the course that other options exist. In other words, collect information that will help you make an educated guess on which content is most likely to be "officially" designated in the future. Choose the most promising content to feature, but still include multiple perspectives and solutions within your formal course content.

Noted

The credibility and relevance of your course can be intensified if you at least mention these multiple perspectives during the course—even if it is just in a very general sense. One exercise you can try for content that has differing perspectives is to ask learners to share what they do in their locations and then verbally compare and contrast their solution to the other solutions discussed in class. This should help to strengthen the relevance of the course. By officially recognizing that other options exist, and providing an opportunity to talk about them, you appear to be "in the know" (even if you weren't totally!).

Challenge: You Have a Global Training Audience

There are a few things that can be a challenge if you have a global training audience. The most obvious, of course, is language difficulties. You may have learners and instructors who speak different languages. With a global audience you have different cultures and norms that you will need to take into account. In addition, with an global audience there can be different tools, work standards, and operational processes in different locations. Developing a course that taps into all these and is still relevant to the entire target audience can be a challenge.

In these situations, you can do the following:

Gain a broad perspective. It is very easy when developing training to get caught up in the best practices of one person or one location. While it can be helpful to work closely with one or two SMEs, it is important that you still gain a broad perspective by talking to multiple people. Find out what employees face in all locations, not just one. Try to secure a list of the products used and the tasks or job operations performed in different locations. Allow for review of material from many different SMEs with different perspectives and situations. Remember that different locations and countries have different norms, rules, and laws regarding the way that work gets done.

Modularize your training. Consider offering a solid baseline training module with additional add-on modules that can be given or not given depending on the location. This will allow you to provide a consistent base module, with location-specific fit-for-purpose add-ons.

Assist nonnative speakers. When you have nonnative speakers in your class, you can do the following things:

- Spell out acronyms.
- Recognize that language learning happens over time.
- Advise the instructor to be available to the participants.
- Be aware of cultural norms that may prevent learners from fully participating. If you are breaking cultural norms within a class, make sure that the instructor explicitly has a conversation about this with the learners.
- Keep a list of vocabulary words that nonnative speakers are likely to have trouble with and clarify those words at the beginning and throughout the class.
- Provide written materials to the learners.
- Allow participants who speak the same language to work in groups together.
- Create inclusive and culturally sensitive course materials. Build exercises into the class that help you reach all learners. For example, if you are dealing with a culture in which a participant would feel rude raising his or her hand, instead of just asking for comments, ask participants to write down questions or answers on a piece of paper first and then go over all of these questions together.

Noted

One of the largest challenges facing our international company is training that needs to be conducted across multiple cultures and languages. Inventive solutions are necessary in addition to the obvious and costly language text translations or live translators during training. A best practice approach is to develop a student manual that augments your training. A nonnative speaker of your language has a reference to translate, study, and refer to when using your training on the job. One step further is to index your presentation, ordinarily slides, to the pages of the manual. The nonnative speaking student can better follow your speaking knowledge transfer with the additional text in the manual.

—Patty Murdock, Technical Training Manager, Schlumberger, Houston, Texas

Challenge: Technology Keeps Changing

I once slaved to put together a course that, upon completion, was promptly obsoleted. The company I was working for decided it was no longer going to offer the main tool covered in the training course. Numerous hours and resources were spent developing courseware that was not going to be used. This was not good.

By its nature, technology will continue to change. This is not a bad thing for the organization. But it can be a challenge when we are trying to keep our training courses up-to-date.

In these situations, you can do the following:

Ask questions. You won't always know if a product is going to go away, but you can at least protect yourself by asking as many questions as you can about the future of the product line. In this rapidly changing marketplace, it is important that training be clued in to which tools or services the business plans to emphasize and which ones it plans to obsolete. Sending out an email to management, engineering, operations, and so forth asking about these things can clue you in to the future of that product line and save you time, resources, and money in the long run.

Be organized. Make sure you are organized and that you know where your sources are. Document what information you received, from whom, and when so that you will have this information available in the event that questions arise about the course content.

Create flexible materials. Design your materials so that they can be easily updated. Create a permanent core of the class that is unchanging technology, and then have add-on modules or handouts that can be given to cover new, constantly changing technology.

Use general exercises. Consider using Category A exercises that ask general questions that are likely to remain relevant as technology evolves. That way you can at least keep the same learner materials as the technology changes. With general exercises in the learner's manual, the only course material that changes with the changing technology will be the instructor's answer key.

Refer learners to "living" locations. Instead of providing the material in hard copy in the class, refer learners to electronic locations where the "living" information resides. This is good because rather than participating in the constant rat race of updating your materials, you are instead leading the learners to the places they can find information on their own.

Summing It Up—A Final Word on Technical Training Basics

Technical training development is a complex, challenging, unique, misunderstood, and sometimes frustrating process. As a nontechnical course developer, you will sometimes find your job to be especially tricky: You must develop courseware using words and concepts you don't fully understand.

The first step to successful development is ensuring that the necessary roles of the development team are covered: that is, making sure the team includes a developer, who is responsible for course structure, organization, and learning theory, and an SME, who is responsible for the technical content within that course structure. Whether the same person performs both roles or whether multiple people perform both roles isn't important. What is important is that each role is given its due diligence. Both roles are necessary for success.

Because quality, health, safety, and the environment are integral factors in the business world, effective training is a must. Launching your technical training project in a comprehensive way helps to ensure that you are meeting the business goals of your organization and addressing the needs of your target audience. Asking the right questions in your initial course design meeting not only helps to accomplish this, but also helps you to create a plan, or a roadmap, of the course for both you and your SME.

Besides objectives, the target audience, and a working title, your course design document should contain a topical outline, organized appropriately. There are benefits and drawbacks to various organizational structures. You will need to look at your specific topic and course objectives in order to determine which structure is ideal.

Gathering information for your technical training project is another necessary, but challenging, aspect of technical course development. In general, you should first catalogue information you have, thinking about it in terms of the "types" of information (for example, categories, levels of information, definitions, components, relationships, analogies, and processes). You need to access as many internal and external sources of information as you can find. When you do find a valid source of information that helps to meet course objectives in some way, you should maximize this material and organize it in a logical manner.

The most important source you have is your SME. It cannot be emphasized enough that being able to work effectively with your SME is a critical skill for a nontechnical person designing a highly technical training course. In highly technical, highly specialized trades, there is not necessarily a library where you can go to find information or to find the answers to your questions. You are dependent on another person, an expert, to provide this information to you. Therefore, your relationship with this person and your communication with this person are very important. As such, when you are designing technical training classes, communication skills become just as important as knowing instructional design theory.

There are various tactics that can be utilized to draw information from and review material with your SME. You will find, however, that what works for one project and one SME does not always work for your next project and your next SME. It is through constant and effective communication with your SME that you are likely to find the right fit for both of you each time.

Sound instructional principles still apply even when a topic is highly technical. A complicated topic does not mean it is OK for the instruction to include only a PowerPoint lecture. There are a variety of exercises that can be included to break up the lecture and help further course objectives; basically, incorporating a variety of useful, relevant, and challenging exercises increases the value of technical training.

The final stage of technical training development is piloting the course and saying good-bye to the project. The pilot course is an opportunity to test your development project. As the pilot course proceeds, you should be analyzing objectives, content, areas for interactivity, participant reactions, questions, and extra things the instructor says. In addition, before you say good-bye to the project, you should put some steps in place so that your material can be more easily updated and kept relevant.

Technical training development is not for the faint of heart. Technical topics are complicated, and developing training for that content can be even more complex. Sometimes you can't tell what content is "nice to know" and what is "need to know." Sometimes your SME has a full-time job outside of the training department or disagrees with other SMEs. Sometimes a project lags or you are tasked with unrealistic deadlines. Sometimes the course you have been asked to redesign has already been taught for years, you have a global training audience, or you are faced with ever-changing technology. Sometimes the organization doesn't understand active training or you don't know how to make the content interactive. Sometimes equipment will be unavailable for training, and sometimes concrete answers do not exist.

Still, whether it be finding a reliable SME, making the course applicable to all locations, incorporating interactivity, keeping the main point of the course in focus, staying up-to-date with changes in the business, or even just learning the eccentric acronyms of the trade you are writing about, there are strategies available to assist you in development.

Getting It Done

As a nontechnical developer, you bring a fresh perspective to the material. Your role is essential to ensure that the structure of the training course meets both organizational and learner needs.

As mentioned earlier, technical training development is a complex, challenging, unique, misunderstood, and sometimes frustrating process. But it is also a process that is necessary and important to today's technical organizations.

With a little focus and preparation, you can effectively develop your own technical training project. Go forth, create, and produce. You can do it.

Worksheet 9–1. Challenges and Solutions

List the challenges you have faced with technical training development. Then, brainstorm possible solutions you will try.

Challenges	Solutions

Appendix

The Developer's Dream: A Fairy-Tale Technical Training Project

∎∎∎

Even though there are a lot of challenges associated with technical training development, with practice, you can streamline your processes and more efficiently and effectively develop your own training courses.

The following is an example of a positive work flow:

Development Notes

Once upon a time in the technical training world, a project began. Today I received a course starter packet from Marie, an SME putting together a training course for a nuclear engineering lab.

I met with Marie. I described our different roles in the project, what the instructional design process entails, and what type of information I would be seeking. We talked about the overall business need of the training course and the audience. From there, we put together preliminary course objectives. Marie wanted to think further on what we did so far. We planned to meet at the end of the week.

I had an extensive meeting with Marie today. She brought a few changes she had made to the objectives, and then we started to brainstorm on topics of the course that would meet those objectives. We took those topics and wrote each one down on an index card. I gave her a brief rundown of the various ways that we could organize technical courses. She thought it would be best to order the course as follows: (1) Basic Knowledge; (2) Pre-job; (3) Job; and (4) Post-job. We then started arranging the index cards in that order. When Marie and I were satisfied that we had included all of the necessary topics, we started to brainstorm activities. At first, when prompted to think about what the learners would be asked to do in class, Marie thought it would be enough to include an informal question-and-answer session halfway through the class at the end of Day 1. I showed her some examples of exercises I had developed for previous courses. Marie looked at them with interest and chose four of them that she thought would work for our topic. I showed her three other exercise examples that I saw as possibilities for our topic, and she agreed to give them a try. We now have a good mix of lecture and activity in most of the class except in the "Job" chapter. We agreed that we will both think further on this. We then quickly looked at our list of topics, and I asked Marie to identify any areas where new graphics, video, models, or animations might be needed. She identified two new images and one animation that were needed. I documented these. At the end of the meeting, I agreed to type out a course design document for Marie to review. She agreed to start gathering technical data she has on her computer and on the lab's server for me. We planned to meet next week.

I emailed the course design document to Marie.

Marie returned the course design document. She slightly tweaked a few terms I used, but the topical outline is still largely the same. Along with the course design document, she sent me seven PowerPoint presentations that she gave to the lab techs last year. Marie explained that two of the presentations clearly fit into the "Basic Knowledge" category, three fit into the "Job" category, and two fit into the "Pre-job" category. I created electronic files on my computer with the names of the four chapters of the course, and placed the seven PowerPoint presentations in their respective folders.

I reviewed the PowerPoint presentations. The "Basic Knowledge" presentations seemed to get really complicated, really fast. I sent Marie an email asking her if she knew of any other sources where I might find some really basic, basic information. Marie responded, giving me the name of an industry association and a government website. I studied these, and the topic made a little more sense to me.

I began to take information from the PowerPoint and put it into the learner manual. After I had done all that I could on my own (based on the outline), Marie and I met and together went through the presentations and continued to add more information. Marie said that in a few days she would email me the exercises we talked about when creating our course design document. Marie cut the meeting short slightly because she had to prepare a presentation for a global product line meeting that she has been asked to attend.

It has been three days since our last meeting, and I still have not heard from Marie regarding information for the exercises. I gave her a call and asked her about the progress of the exercises. She seemed a little confused and asked me to describe again what I needed. I explained the exercises again and advised her that I would send her some documents that should help remind her of the information I needed. I prepared skeleton worksheets for Marie to fill out that would eventually become the exercises of the class. I emailed these worksheets to Marie.

I formatted and rewrote the existing PowerPoint text that is now incorporated into the learner manual. The learner manual chapters begin to take shape. After I completed each chapter, I sent it to Marie to review.

Marie and I met to go over the three chapters that she has edited so far: Basic Knowledge, Pre-job, and Job. She explained each of her comments to me to my satisfaction. I agreed to make her content edits, and she agreed that she will continue to edit the final chapter.

I sent Marie an email asking if she has completed the skeleton worksheets for our course exercises. Marie immediately responded and said she had all of the worksheets completed except for one, because she was trying to get clarification about a particular field test. I asked her to send me what is already complete. She agreed, and after I received the files, I formatted the exercises.

Marie sent me the last chapter. Marie was preparing to travel internationally and informed me she would not be available for a face-to-face meeting until late next week. She said there are only a few changes needed in the Post-job chapter and thought that we could simply discuss these over the phone tomorrow in order to keep things moving.

Marie and I talked over the phone and went over her edits from the last chapter. The changes were pretty self-explanatory, so it was a short conversation. She updated me on the still-missing information she needed to complete the last exercise worksheet. She said she thought she should have an answer after this international trip.

During her trip, Marie emailed me the final worksheet. She also explained that a pilot course has already been scheduled for three weeks from now, and that she would actually be teaching it. We coordinated to meet after she returned to go over the class as a whole.

I finished making all the edits to the final chapter. I incorporated the missing exercise information and finalized the content.

Marie and I met for a course debrief. We went over the course as a whole and the sections, one by one. I asked if she had any questions. She had a couple about one of the exercises. I explained the directions to her as if I were speaking directly to the learners. She said, "Ahhhhh" and commented that she now understood. I explained that if there were any problems I would be attending the pilot course and would stand up to help explain the exercises if necessary. Marie looked relieved and thanked me.

The pilot course was held. Marie did not tell the learners that it was a pilot course, preferring to get unbiased feedback. The course ran smoothly for the most part. After the class, we discussed with the learners what they liked and disliked about the course. There was one exercise in the Job chapter that needed to be reworked, and there was a chart in the Pre-job section that needed to be replaced. We celebrated after the class.

I made the necessary tweaks to the course and sent them to Marie. She responded that the changes looked good. I then set up an electronic folder for Marie to log any additional changes she thought about as she continued to teach the course. I thanked her for her time and she thanked me for my time.

We both lived happily ever after with the finished product.

The End

Smooth projects like this do occur in real life. It can, and it will, eventually happen to you!

References and Resources

Astleitner, H. 2005. "Principles of Effective Instruction—General Standards for Teachers and Instructional Designers." *Journal of Instructional Psychology 32*(1): 3–8.

Carnegie, D. 1936. *How to Win Friends and Influence People*. New York: Simon & Schuster.

Felder, R.M. and R. Brent. 2005. "Understanding Student Differences." *Journal of Engineering Education 94*(1): 57–72.

Felder, R.M. and L.K. Silverman. 1988. "Learning and Teaching Styles in Engineering Education." *Engineering Education 78*(7): 674–681.

Graaff, E., G. Saunders-Smits, and M. Nieweg. 2005. *Research and Practice of Active Learning in Engineering Education*. Amsterdam, NL: Pallus Publications–Amsterdam University Press.

Hannum, W. 2009. "Training Myths: False Beliefs that Limit the Efficiency and Effectiveness of Training Solutions, Part 1." *Performance Improvement 48*(2): 26–30.

Hargis, G., M. Carey, A. Hernandez, P. Hughes, D. Longo, S. Rouiller, and E. Wilde. 2004. *Developing Quality Technical Information: A Handbook for Writers and Editors* (2nd Edition). Upper Saddle River, NJ: Prentice Hall.

Hodell, C. 2000. *ISD From the Ground Up*. Alexandria, VA: ASTD Press.

Lalley, J. and R. Miller. 2007. "The Learning Pyramid: Does It Point Teachers in the Right Direction?" *Education and Information Technologies 128*(1): 64–79.

Meier, D. 2000. *The Accelerated Learning Handbook: A Creative Guide to Designing and Delivering Faster, More Effective Training Programs*. New York: McGraw-Hill.

Murdock, B.B. 1962. "The Serial Position Effect of Free Recall." *Journal of Experimental Psychology 64*(5): 482–488.

Murdock, P., K. Pigusch, S. Matta, and S. Wakefield. 2011. *Improving Technical Oilfield Training: Interactive Classroom Techniques*. Paper SPE 142203 prepared for presentation at the Health, Safety, Security and Environmental Conference, Houston, Texas, United States, 21–23 March. doi: 10.2118/142203-MS.

Nayak, S. 2006. "The Broken Lecture: An Innovative Method of Teaching." *Advances in Physiology Education* 30: 135–140.

Patterson, K., J. Grenny, R. McMillan, and A. Switzler. 2002. *Crucial Conversations: Tools for Talking When Stakes Are High*. New York: McGraw-Hill.

Patterson, K., J. Grenny, R. McMillan, and A. Switzler. 2005. *Crucial Confrontations: Tools for Resolving Broken Promises, Violated Expectations, and Bad Behavior*. New York: McGraw-Hill.

Wakefield, S. and S. Matta. 2010. *Alternative Training Tactics Provide Deeper Understanding of PDM Principles for Field Operators*. Paper SPE 132409 presented at the SPE Annual Technical Conference and Exhibition, Florence, Italy, 19–22 September. doi: 10.2118/132409-MS.

Wakefield, S. and K. Pigusch. 2010. *BHA and Drill String Fundamentals: Technology Training for Beginners*. Paper SPE 131922 presented at the SPE Asia Pacific Oil & Gas Conference and Exhibition, Brisbane, Queensland, Australia, 18–20 October. doi: 10.2118/131922-MS.

About the Author

Sarah Wakefield is a Technical Training Supervisor for Schlumberger Limited in Houston, Texas. Her primary responsibility is managing the design and development of technical training courses for audiences in locations such as the United States, Europe, South America, the Middle East, Russia, China, and North Africa. Before this, Sarah worked as a curriculum designer and technical writer for various organizations. Sarah also was an instructor of communication, writing, and "life success" courses at Ivy Tech State College and at Purdue University in Fort Wayne, Indiana. Sarah holds a master's degree in communication from Purdue, as well as a bachelor's degree from Purdue with a double major in professional writing and psychology.

Index

THE *ASTD* MISSION:

Empower professionals to develop knowledge and skills successfully.

The American Society for Training & Development provides world-class professional development opportunities, content, networking, and resources for workplace learning and performance professionals.

Dedicated to helping members increase their relevance, enhance their skills, and align learning to business results, ASTD sets the standard for best practices within the profession.

The society is recognized for shaping global discussions on workforce development and providing the tools to demonstrate the impact of learning on the organizational bottom line. ASTD represents the profession's interests to corporate executives, policy makers, academic leaders, small business owners, and consultants through world-class content, convening opportunities, professional development, and awards and recognition.

Resources
- *T+D (Training + Development)* Magazine
- ASTD Press
- Industry Newsletters
- Research and Benchmarking
- Representation to Policy Makers

Networking
- Local Chapters
- Online Communities
- ASTD Connect
- Benchmarking Forum
- Learning Executives Network

Professional Development
- Certificate Programs
- Conferences and Workshops
- Online Learning
- CPLP™ Certification Through the ASTD Certification Institute
- Career Center and Job Bank

Awards and Best Practices
- ASTD BEST Awards
- Excellence in Practice Awards
- E-Learning Courseware Certification (ECC) Through the ASTD Certification Institute

Learn more about ASTD at www.astd.org.
1.800.628.2783 (U.S.) or 1.703.683.8100
customercare@astd.org

031130.62220